Jean Claude

Cruel Persecutions of the Protestants in the Kingdom of France

Jean Claude

Cruel Persecutions of the Protestants in the Kingdom of France

ISBN/EAN: 9783337243289

Printed in Europe, USA, Canada, Australia, Japan

Cover: Foto ©ninafisch / pixelio.de

More available books at **www.hansebooks.com**

CRUEL PERSECUTIONS

OF THE

PROTESTANTS

IN THE

KINGDOM OF FRANCE

FIRST AMERICAN REPRINT

OF THE ENGLISH TRANSLATION

PUBLISHED IN LONDON IN 1707

WITH A BIOGRAPHICAL SKETCH OF THE AUTHOR

JEAN CLAUDE

BY

NARCISSE CYR,

PUBLISHER

BOSTON,
1893

TO THE

REV. CHARLES CHINIQUY,

THE

Venerable and Eloquent Champion

OF

EVANGELICAL CHRISTIANITY,

WHO

DURING MANY YEARS OF ARDUOUS LABORS AND FREQUENT
PERSECUTIONS, HAS NOT ONLY EXPOSED

THE ERRORS OF ROME,

BUT BROUGHT THOUSANDS OF SOULS TO JESUS CHRIST.

THIS FIRST AMERICAN REPRINT

OF THE

ENGLISH TRANSLATIONS OF CLAUDE'S MASTERPIECE IS
RESPECTFULLY DEDICATED

BY

NARCISSE CYR.

CLAUDE AND HIS MASTERPIECE.

The author of this remarkable book, which is offered to the American public for the first time, is Jean Claude, one of the most eloquent French Protestant ministers, and certainly the ablest defender of the Reformed Faith in the 17th century. After he was called to the church at Charenton—a parish which included the Protestants of Paris and vicinity—he became the natural champion of Protestantism in France, and fought valiantly against such men as Arnauld, Nicole and Bossuet, who was then the *Goliath* of Rome.

Our author was born, in 1619, at Sauvetat, a small town near. Agen, in the Southwest of France. His father was a Protestant pastor, who attended himself to the early education of his son. The latter after going through the usual course of study, was ordained at the age of twenty-six, and called first to the little church of La Freyne. He remained there only one year, having been promoted to a

more important pastorate, that of the church
of Sainte Affrique. After eight years of
faithful work in that old interesting town,
he was invited to the church at Nimes, then,
as now, the most important outside of Paris.
This call was highly complimentary as well
as very encouraging to the comparatively
young pastor. He was then thirty-five, a
good age to assume important and responsible
duties.

In the city of Nimes, Claude found more
ample opportunities to develop his talents for
the pulpit. A daily preaching service was held
in the church, each of the three pastors officiat-
ing in turn; the children were taught carefully
the principles of Evangelical Christianity, thor-
oughly catechized, in the first and best sense of
the word, as they are still by the French pastors; moreover, the sick and feeble of the flock
were cared for and protected from Romish
proselytism. Such a pastorate, we can easily
understand, involved duties which greatly taxed
the time and strength of Claude; yet he chose
to add to them the voluntary work of private
lectures to the students of the Protestant Liter-
ary and Theological Academy in that city,
lectures which were very much appreciated by
these students for the ministry.

Claude was not only an eloquent preacher

and a faithful pastor, but a man of strong convictions and a bold defender of what he considered the truth. So that when a Protestant, whom the court had gained to the idea of a Reunion of the Protestants with the Catholics, appeared in a Synod of the Lower Languedoc, to advocate that plan, Claude opposed it with energy and ability. He was successful, and for that *offence* punished by a Decree of the Council, which forbade him to exercise the ministry in that Province of which Nimes was the capital.

Claude immediately went to Paris to appeal from this arbitrary decree; he remained there six months, but his efforts were unsuccessful. His residence in the Metropolis, however, was useful to him in more ways than one. He became better acquainted with some of his distinguished co-religionists, as well as with the enemies of the Protestant faith. He was doubtless invited to preach at Charenton, and thus the way was prepared for his call to that charge two or three years later.

When Claude became convinced that there was no justice to be obtained from the government, he returned to the south of France, and was soon called to the important church of Montauban, which he served faithfully until

1666, when he accepted the most responsible post, that of Charenton.

Even under the reign of toleration, secured to them by the Edict of Nantes, the Huguenots were not allowed to have a place of worship in Paris, nor within five miles of that city. At first, and for many years, they were obliged to have their church at the little town of Ablon, about eight miles from the capital, a place not at all central for them. After many petitions and supplications, they were permitted to exchange Ablon for Charenton, which is precisely five miles southeast of Paris. There a place of worship, a *Temple*, as it was called, was constructed by the famous architect, DeBrosses. It was a plain building, but well adapted to the wants of the Protestants of the Metropolis and vicinity. Fourteen thousand persons could be seated in it, and the three pastors who ministered to that parish, scattered over a large extent of country, preached in turn eloquent and earnest sermons to interested audiences; hearers who came five, ten and even fifteen miles to hear the Evangel of light and life, which the glorious Reformation had restored to the world.

It was from this large, appreciative and beloved flock that the eminent pastor was torn away, on the very day that the Edict of Revocation was registered in the Parliament of Paris. The Court would not grant him the fifteen days allowed by the Edict to all the ministers, without distinction, but as soon as this document was published in the Metropolis, Claude was "commanded to leave Paris within four and twenty hours, and forthwith to depart the Kingdom. For this end they put him into the hands of one of the King's footmen, with orders not to leave him till he was out of his dominions." He took the coach at Paris, the next day, for Brussells, with his escort, who, it is said, was very civil to him all the way to the frontier, where they separated. The criminal, of whom France was not worthy, had evidently made a very favorable impression upon the royal servant.

It is interesting to know that the senior pastor of Charenton, as he journeyed through France, received many marks of kindness, not only from his brethren, but even from some of his enemies.

From Brussells, Claude proceeded to Holland, where many distinguished exiles had preceded him. He met there with a warm reception from his fellow countrymen and the inhabitants of that hospitable country. He was honored soon after his arrival with a considerable pension by William, the Prince of Orange, a fact which shows in what high estimation this Huguenot pastor was held. Thus relieved from pecuniary anxiety, the old soldier of Christ who had fought valiantly all his life in favor of the Reformed Religion, could at last enjoy days of a well deserved and much needed rest. He was then sixty-six years of age. For men like our author there is little respite in this world, where they see so much work to be done. While Claude found in Holland a very congenial society—for that country had really become a great intellectual and religious center for the French Protestants—his heart was in France, with his suffering brethren, and he soon concluded that he could not better serve the cause of religious Freedom, Humanity and Justice, than by publishing to the world the details of the cruel persecutions which had preceded and followed the Revocation of the Edict of Nantes, protesting before Heaven and Earth against all the violences, persecutions and horrors perpetrated by the agents of Louis XIV, at the instigation of Père La Chaise, Le Tellier and other Jesuits.

"This book, written in French, which was then the language not only of diplomacy and of courts, but also that of all educated people, was destined to be widely read and to awaken deep sympathy for the persecuted Huguenots while showing the persecutors in their true light. As well says Prof. Henry M. Baird, of the University of the City of New York, "it was the most scathing indictment which that generation knew of the atrocities perpetrated by Louis XIV., and it produced such a sensation as did no other book. Louis himself winced under the lash, and desired to destroy every copy of the book he could lay hand upon. It is no wonder that he persuaded the weak king of England to cause it to be burned by the public hangman of the city of London. To us this is a recommendation."

It is worthy of notice that the spies of the French monarch had discovered that a translation of this book into English was being made and would soon be published. The French embassador in London hastened to inform James II of the fact, and denounced the work as a most abominable production, not only full of slanders against his royal master, but also of republican and revolutionary ideas! The king of England showed great readiness to please his brother monarch, and immediately ordered the book to be suppressed and the printer punished. All the copies of the translation that could be found, were immediately seized and burnt publicly, by the hangman, in the court of the Royal Exchange of the English capital! As for the publisher, although the work bore no name, he was soon discovered by the spies of Rome, imprisoned and financially ruined. The translator was also severely punished. And yet these two men had omitted the most forcible passages of Claude's masterpiece, in fact nearly a third of the work, so as to evade prosecution from the government. What would have been their fate, had they published the book as it was in 1707 and now with its strong but well merited denunciations of the most outrageous persecutions that Christians ever suffered, with its mighty protests against the horrors perpetrated in the name of religion, and with its most touching appeals to the conscience of Europe, and to the entire world?

Thank God, the government which burnt Claude's book, disappeared two years later, and a new era dawned for England when William of Orange landed on the British Isle, accompanied by his Huguenot regiments, his best and most heroic soldiers.

Claude, alas, was not privileged to hail that glorious day, but he lived long enough to see of the fruits of his last labors in behalf of his persecuted brethren, and his end was peace and joy. Having been called to deliver the sermon on Christmas, 1666, he preached with his ordinary unction. The Princess of Orange was

present and enjoyed the discourse as usual.
The preacher was apparently well, but that
very day was taken ill and died on the 13th of
January following. Not much is known of his
illness, but enough to warrant the statement
that he died a most edifying death, sustained
by that Faith, " which is the substance of things
hoped for, the evidence of things unseen."

Claude, by giving the details of the cruel
persecutions suffered by the French Protestants at the close of the 17th century, has left
to the world a legacy, whose value can hardly
be overestimated. His graphic account has
stirred the hearts of thousands in Europe and
will have the same effect in America. The
reprint of this book has been greatly encouraged
by a number of our representative men in this
country who have become acquainted with its
contents. It comes opportunely with its les-
sons and warnings at the present time. The
learned Prof. Coussirat, of the Presbyterian
College of Montreal, a descendant of the
Huguenots, did not exaggerate the importance
of the present reprint when he wrote to the
undersigned : " You are doing a good work in
showing free American citizens what they may
expect, should the Catholic church ever obtain
supremacy in the United States." He further
called attention to a fact, too much overlooked

in this country, saying: "It is certain that Rome has never repudiated the acts of her agents, nor has she ever given up her pretended right to coerce those whom she stigmatizes as heretics. God grant that Claude's *Plaintes des Protestants* may be a warning to Americans!"

NARCISSE CYR.

A
SHORT ACCOUNT
Of the COMPLAINTS,
AND
Cruel PERSECUTIONS
OF THE
PROTESTANTS
IN THE
KINGDOM of FRANCE.

LONDON,
Printed by W. REDMAYNE. 1707.

TO THE

MOST REVEREND

FATHER IN GOD,

His Grace the Lord Archbishop

OF

CANTERBURY,

And the Right Reverend Father
in God the Lord Bishop

OF

LONDON.

MY LORDS,

I have newly caused to be translated
into English the Book intituled, THE COM-
PLAINTS OF THE PROTESTANTS IN THE
KINGDOM OF FRANCE with this design, to

let Great Britain know and understand by
Examples, how it is that Popery, when it
has the power on its Side uses to proceed
against all them that are not of its own
Communion; and how much this united
Kingdom is therefore indebted to the
Divine Goodness, for having both hitherto
preserved, and for Posterity also secured
it from those great Evils, which so considerable a Part of those professing with
them the same Holy Faith have suffered,
and still do suffer, in other Parts.

This YOUR LORDSHIPS know per-
fectly well; and have no need to be told it
over again;   But the Generality of People
in this Nation are greatly Ignorant in this
Matter, and can hardly be persuaded to
believe the Excess, Violence and Barbarity
which by our Enemies has been and still is
used.   Wherefore for the Information of
such, and for the disappointment of the
Emissaries of France, who would gladly
have the Remembrance hereof to be lost;
I have thought it might be very proper to
address to YOUR LORDSHIPS the Part
I have in this valuable Piece; which is the

Translation of it; and lay before your Eyes the matters which it contains, both because 'tis well known how your LORD-SHIPS have, as with all your might, so with a Success answerable, labored to dissipate the Storm, which lately seem'd to gather here, and threaten this flourishing Kingdom with the like Calamities: And how you have moreover greatly refreshed and comforted the FRENCH PROTESTANTS, who fled hither for Refuge, as became true FATHERS IN CHRIST.

YOUR LORDSHIPS are not ignorant, how they then made their Complaints, and their Protestations against the persecution of France: Nor can it be a Secret to you what was done here, consequently to the publishing this true and faithful Memorial of theirs, to give a just Representation of their State. But the Copies hereof were not only suppressed, but prohibited so strictly, and in such a manner watch'd as they were hardly ever known to this Nation, as I can find. And hence it is that the very Children of the Refugees themselves, who either came hither very

young, or else are born here, do not know
the Cause of the Exile and Transmigration
of their Fathers and Mothers; a thing
which they certainly ought to be well informed of, and never to forget.   It is with
a Prospect of perpetuating to future Gen-
erations the sad Remembrance of the Sub-
version of the State and Condition of the
Protestants of France, by the unjust Revocation of the Edict of Nantes, that one
who is a refugee here has caused the said
Book, containing their Complaints and
Protestations to be reprinted for all the
rest.

And whereas by a Declaration of King
Charles II. of the 28th of July, 1681,
YOUR LORDSHIPS are marked out ex-
presly by the Dignities of the Archbishop
of CANTERBURY and the Bishop of LON-
DON, on purpose to receive the Petitions
and Complaints of the distressed Refugees,
in order to be communicated as need shall
require; YOUR LORDSHIPS are therefore humbly supplicated to cast your Eyes
upon the Preface of this Book, which
showes the several Estates of these poor

persecuted People, as it is at present, to which either by the Lapse of Time, or by the Juncture of War, or both, great Numbers of them have been reduced.

The poor among them are hence forc'd to cry again for your Help at this time: And they presume also to promise themselves the same from your great Charity, and that from you, HER MAJESTY shall be informed of the pressing Necessity there is to recommend it to her British Parliament, in Order to the Relief of their extreme Poverty and Indigence. And this they are the more encouraged to, since under the late Reign the House of Commons did make no Scruple to acknowledge, and publicly notify, that all things consider'd these Poor were not any charge at all to the Nation: And since that the House of Lords also under the present happy Reign of her Majesty has declar'd to the Kingdom that the foreign Protestants are profitable to it.

Nevertheless, the Old, the Sick, the Widows, the Orphans, and all those who are uncapable among them to get their

Livelihood, being by long Continuance of the Persecution in the Country of their Nativity left destitute of everything, do here implore as with one common Voice the Pity of YOUR LORDSHIPS, and beseech your Help, so far at least as to request in their Favour from this charitable Nation the Conveniences of Life in so abounding a Country as this, where Providence has cast them.* And for as much as Human Nature has need of being sustained by Food and raiment no less in time of War than in time of Peace,

*Your Lordship, will see their Number, Names, Ages, Qualities and Habitations by a New List that is a making.

they hope that YOUR LORDSHIPS will be pleased, notwithstanding the great Occasions of the Nation, to solicit for them the Means whereby they may subsist, both now and hereafter; as being Objects spoil'd of their Goods, and all they had in the World, who have been constrained to forsake their ungrateful Country, because they would not bow the Knee to Baal.

For these Reasons and the Royal Declaration that I alledge, which never has been

altered, I take the Liberty to put this
Book, which contains a short but faithful
Recital of Matter of Fact, under the Protection of the Two most worthy Prelates
of Europe. All the Refugees have experienced in general the Effects of your
Christian Compassion and Generosity.:
They desire gratefully to acknowledge as
much, both before God and before the
World. What you, my Lords, have done
for them so honourably, and so piously,
they must all with one Mouth and one
Heart needs own and confess. May
YOUR LORDSHIPS continue to them
always the same Good Will and Affection,
and also survive their Miseries.

Now I cannot here mention their Ac-
knowledgements, without being oblig'd to
speak at the same time of your Benefac-
tions: And here indeed would be the
Place to publish them to the World, for
the Promotion of Piety and Charity; but
this I dare not undertake, but shall leave
to some others to perform who can do it
better. In the mean while least my
Silence on this Head might be of bad Con-

sequence and Example, I could not but give this small Hint: Tho' I forbear, YOUR LORDSHIPS may be assured there is no person has a deeper Sense than I of your eminent Qualities and Services in Favour both of Religion and of the State ; and am not the less for concealing my name.

YOUR LORDSHIPS,

Most Humble
Faithful and
Obedient Servant.

THE
PREFACE.

This Book was first published in French in the Year 1686, and then Translated into English; a Copy whereof a Merchant of *London* sent to one of his brothers in *France;* and some time after acquainted him, that upon the instances of the French Ambassador at this Court, the same had been order'd to be burnt, and the Translator and Printer thereof almost ruin'd by Imprisonments and Fines, and that the Papists took a great deal of Care to suppress all the Copies, least the Nation should be made acquainted with the Truths contained therein; where the Cruelties exercis'd against the Protestants of *France*, who would not abjure their Religion, and embrace the Romish, are so truly represented: 'Twas at the same time that Preparations were making in order to put the same methods in practice against the Protestants in *England*, where the Pope kept openly a Nuncio, besides several Monks and Jesuits: There were also several Writers, as Sir Roger L'Estrange and others, imploy'd, and well paid, to assert that there was no Persecution in *France*, but contrariwise voluntary Conversions to the Romish Religion; And that as to the great number of People who left their Country to come over into this, under pretence of Religion, they did it only for private ends and self interest. But these Impostures were soon born down by the sight of so many poor Wretches that throng'd hither for Refuge from those dreadful calamities which were inflicted on them; The consideration of which made the Nation seriously think of securing the Protestant Religion, which its Enemies design'd to destroy here as they had done in *France* and elsewhere.

Some Years after, the Gentleman who had received this Book in *English*, came over to augment the number of the Refugees in this Kingdom, and inquiring after it, 'twas impossible for him to light on any other Copy here : But having been told since, that the Anonimous Author, was that Excellent Man of God, the late Mr. *Claude*, Minister of Paris, who died in *Holland* soon after he had written this Book, by this means he got one in *French;* and very lately by the care of a * Reverend Divine, another in English, (perhaps the only one extant,) which being compar'd together, it appears, that the Translator for some regard he had to those times, when the Enemies of our Holy Religion were in great credit did designedly omit several matters of fact, and them the most important to the Cause of the Refugees ; inso-

*Doctor Manningham.

much, that above the fourth part of it was cut off in the Translation; tho' the Translator far'd none the better for it.

Seeing then the great efforts made to suppress this Book, it the rather deserves to be preserv'd among Protestants to all Posterity. And for as much as the Refugees in this Kingdom durst not by reason of the strict Prohibition keep any of them, 'tis thought of the utmost Importance to revive it again, especially at this Juncture, which seems so much more favorable than the former, and to offer it intire as if it were a new Work to the Nation, according to the Refugees first intent, in which view it is now reprinted in both Languages, for the convenience of those that understand but one.

The Public will see that this Book is an Abridgment of the cruel and inhumane Persecution, exercis'd against the Protestants in *France* for several Years together, to the Prejudice of the Edict of *Nantes*, and its dismal consequences to the beginning of the Year 1686. 'Tis likewise a solemn Protestation of above 150,000 Refugees in several Protestant States, who both for themselves and their Brethren, that could not escape the hands of the Dragoons, do call to Heaven and Earth for vengence of the outrages done to them or their Relations, as also for the Cruelties still exercis'd against those that have the misfortune to be yet kept in Prisons, Dungeons, Convents, or Galleys, for the sake of their Religion, to the prejudice of Natural Rights, Treaties, Public Faith, Edicts, Promises and Oaths. 'Tis to be hoped there are other writers since Mr. *Claude*, who will have gather'd together the further Transactions relating to this subject, in order to transmit the Memory thereof to Posterity, inspight of the Disguises and Lies, the Authors of those Evils, and malicious Reports have spread abroad, by means of the Declarations and Subscriptions which they have forc'd from those they persecuted, obliging 'em to say that their pretended Abjurations were voluntary. But these foul Imputations so well known to the Refugees in this Country, obliged them to challenge 'em as false, and to put this Question to their Enemies ; To what purpose (were things as you say) are the Passages by Sea and Land shut up, and guarded with so much Cost and Precution, even against those that have given you such Declarations ? Why are so many Thousands of both Sexes come into this country ? 'Tis well known they will return this Answer, That the loss of those People is but inconsiderable to *France*, since there are only the poorer, and meaner sort that go away, for the Rich are so narrowly watch'd, that they cannot escape : But this is another notorious Falsehood, for on the contary there are in genereal only those who had Money or Credit that could be at the vast Expenses necessary for their Escape, which is computed to amount to at least 200,000 l. Sterling in *specie* paid to the Masters of English ships, merely for the passage of those that came over into this Country; and as for their Quality (without undervaluing in the least any of those that fled into others Countries) there are come hither a Duke, and a Mareschal of *France*, some Generals of Armies, a Dutchess, several Counts and Countesses, Marquises, and Marchionesses, Judges of Soverign Courts, Viscounts, Barons, Noblemen, and Gentlemen, Ladies and Gentlewomen, Men of Learning, Lawyers, Physicians, Substantial Merchants, Tradesmen of all sorts, and many Captains, Masters, Mariners, Gardners, and Husbandmen; besides the great number of Ministers who were banish'd that Kingdom, with orders, to depart forthwith upon pain of the Galleys. These are the Persons who are said to be of little Consequence; whilst their Enemies do say in other places, that the loss is irreparable. Now its plain on the one hand, that the love of

one's Country, Estate, Settlement,
Relations, Friends, plenty of Wine
and other enjoyments of this Life are
very strong tyes; from whence it
must be confess'd on the other hand,
that there must be some stronger
Motives to induce such Multitudes to
forsake all the afore-mentioned Advantages, and seek an *Azilum* in
Foreign-Countries and unknown Languages, against the persecutions of
an ungrateful Country, where one is
not allowed to Worship God according to ones Conscience, as the Author
of this Book has manifestly evidenc'd.
This is nevertheless the dismal Lot
of the Refugees, and were this a
proper Place to speak of the Hazards,
Shipwrecks, and Dangers which so
many Thousands have been expos'd
to, and how many have perish'd before they arriv'd in this free Country,
no doubt but the Reader would
pass a Charitable Judgement upon
those that are come over; But
this would require a Volume by itself;
however, to hear the Emissaries of

Rome, who do not stick impudently to affirm it, one would think there had never been any Persecution in *France,* or at least if there had, that it has ceased, seeing they say, that there are now no Protestants left; which they endeavour the more to insinuate in this time of War, when all Correspondence is intirely cut off. 'Tis therefore the Duty of those that are here, to refute that falsehood, by asserting real and sensible matters of fact, such as may convince the World, and *Great Britain* in particular, that since the Revocation of the Edict of *Nantes*, the Reformed of *France* have continually being persecuted; For, not to speak of the Slaugthers committed in the *Cevennes*, nor of what has passed elsewhere, but only of certain matters of fact which have happened since the Death of the Author of this Book, as may be proved by Persons living here, and transacted in *a little District* of the *Parliament* of *Guienne*, (reputed to be one of the most indulgent of that Kingdom in

point of Religion, by reason of the
Trade of that Country with the
Northern Protestants,) one may there
by judge, whether there is still such a
thing as a Persecution in *France.*
To which end, the Paptists in this
kingdom are desir'd to address themselves to *Martha Guisard* living in
Frith-Street Soho. She will tell them
that she came out of *France,* because
John Guisard her Father was Burnt
at *Nera,* being accused of having ir-
reverently receiv'd the Cost. Let
them speak to Mrs. *Tinel,* Wife of a
French Minster at *Bristol,* and to his
Sister in Law, they will tell them,
that the Sieur * *Mar-
gueron* their Father
was Hang'd at *Ste. Foy,*
for having held a Re-
ligious Assemby in his
House, his Estate was confiscated and
the House pulled down, their Mother
condemned to make *Amende Honourable,* her head shav'd by the Hangman, bare-footed, and in her Shift,
holding in her hand a lighted Torch,

The History of his Edifying Death is to be Sold at the Widow Baldwin in Warwick-Lane.

and afterwards to a perpetual Imprisonment; and that they escaped the like Severities by their flight into this Kingdom, with their Brother since kill'd in Our Army. Let them ask of the Sieur *Peyferie* and his family, what made them a great Estate, to be reduc'd to great Streights in *Tower-street in Soho?* He will answer that being accused with some Neighbours of his, of having exercis'd his Religion in his Country-house, he was condemned to be hang'd, his House demolished, and his Woods destroy'd, but God of his mercy deliver'd him from that danger: Let them inquire of · Mrs. *Charlotte*, and Mrs. Mary, Daughters of the Sieur *de la Ramiers*, who died in the Service of England? They will tell them that his Castle was pull'd down, and his Woods destroy'd, for having held there a Religious Assembly. The Sieurs *Dupre*, and *Moses du Boust*, now living in the Parish of *St. Giles in the Fields*, will testify, that they were persecuted in their Persons and Estates, their

Houses demolished before they fled
into this Country, where they are
necessitated to live upon the Charity
of the Nation, the one being 80 years
old, and the other grown Invalid in
our Army; *Martha Trapeau* and
Mary Labe living in Soho will answer: That being Sick they received a visit from the Priest and Magistrate, to whom they declar'd, that
notwithstanding they had through
their persecution, been forced to abjure their Religion, they were resolv'd
however to die in it; but being re-
covered, they were condemned to
make *Amende Honourable*, and to be
perpetually confined in the Manufac-
ture of *Bourdeaux*, from whence they
made their escape to the great danger
of their Lives. 'Tis into the same
place of Torment that *Olympe Passe-
laigue of Bergerac, Joan Darrat*, and
Joan her Sister of *Faugeroles*, *Joan
Groux, Judith Chabot, Catherine
Mulb*, the two Mrs. *Gorinx, Martha
Cove*, and others now here, to the
number of 18 were confin'd for en-

deavouring to fly from the Persecution, having had the misfortune to be taken going out of *France*, from whence they afterwards made their escape in the Night through the Windows; as for the Men, if any of them are surpris'd making their escape; 'tis *Amende Honourable* and the *Galleys*, and the Sieurs *Constans* and *Bessete of Duras* have undergone that punishment for assisting in the Assembly with the Sieur *Margueron*, and do there keep company to a great many others that suffer Persecution for the Cause of Religion. The Sieur *Augier of Casteljaloux*, who Died in the Fortress of *Blaye*, is also an example of the Rigor exercis'd by the Persecutors.

To shew how they still deal in *France* with the Protestants, here is an undeniable matter of fact, *Mary Perreau* living in Spittlefields, will tell you, that she was married at *Plymouth* to *Peter Perreau* a French Pilot, who a Month after their marriage being Sail'd for the

Straights was taken, and carried into *France*, where he was condemned to the Galleys for 101 Years. Since then as 'tis Death or the Galleys for the Men who refuse to change their Religion, or, are found making their escape, so 'tis *Amende Honourable* and perpetual Imprisonment for the Women, where a great number have Dyed, among others the Illustrious Wife of the Holy Martyr the Sieur *Margueron*, and lately the Confessors Mrs. *La Serre*, and Mrs. *Gentillot;* the Prisons continue still filled with Women, some of which have been above 20 Years in the Town-house of *Bordeaux*, glorifying God by their Sufferings; and amongst others, Mrs. *Villotes* a Gentlewoman of 80 Years of age, that has a Daughther living in Soho, *Claudine le May*, and *Joan* her Daughter, Mrs. *Barbot*, Mrs. *Charlemont*, and a great many more do sufficiently testify, that were it not for the Persecution, so many Persons would hardly be kept in Prison.

These are living Witnesses for

such as desire to be further satisfied
of the Truth, and this small number
(which might be infinitely increased),
its hop'd will suffice both to manifest
the Truth, and to confute the Malice
of those who are endeavouring to
subvert it by their false slanders a-
gainst the Refugees; As for in-
stance they gave out sometime since
that all the Protestants in *France*
went to Mass, and were really converted to the Romish Religion; than
which nothing is more notoriously
false, for proof whereof one needs
only observe, that the present War
having necessitated the raising the
Militia in *France;* Personal Taxes
have been laid on the Protestants
who refuse to go to Mass, which
serves as a Fund for the Payment of
the said Militia. So that the Clergy
of *France*, who had promis'd the
French King to extirpate the Protestant Religion, and to make the
Romish triumph, have done the quite
contrary: For let them Banish the
Ministers, Prohibit the Assemblies,

Exile 'em and inflict even Death itself, if they please, this doth not destroy Religion, but only as it were cuts
off those rivulets whose Springs remain, for they cannot Banish the Light
of the Reform'd, nor hinder the Con-
solation of the Holy Ghost.

But say they, the Persecutors do
not now use Rigors, they will instruct
the Reform'd by Degrees, who being
once well instructed, will have no re-
pugnance to remain in the Romish
Church. This is a great mistake,
the Reformed are not desirous of
Instructions from such Ministers; let
them be told never so often, that
their Ministers have misrepresented
the Romish Religion, and that they
are to harken to their Converters
who will give them a right Information of it, to this they will readily
answer, we are not so to be Instructed by you, for the Edicts and Declarations you have obtained from the
King against us, our Ministers Banish'd at your sollicitations our Brethren condemned to the Galleys, and

to Death by your Persecutions, the Cruelties exercis'd against us by the Dragoons, all your Treacheries, Injustices, and Cruelties do sufficiently shew us what your Religion and Faith is, and plainly convinces us, that it is not from God, what Profession soever you pretend to make of Christianity. Let this suffice to be said in justification of the Protestants that still remain in *France*, under the longest and sharpest Persecution that ever was heard of, and in which Fraud and Imposture are countenanced by force, and this is the reason the matters of fact here-mentioned have been produced from one little part of the Kingdom only, because they may so easily be proved here *Viva Voce*. And then let any one judge what is transacted in other Places, where the Protestants are us'd with greater severity. And by the way one may here see the Causes and Motives, of the depopulating of *France*, and the Reasons why so many Thousands fled into Protestant Countries to shelter themselves, from the Injuries their Brethren are still expos'd to.

Having now represented the several Qualities of the French Refugees in this Kingdom, (who must not be suppos'd to be of higher rank than those that have taken Sanctuary in other Countries), it may confidently be affirm'd that such an encrease of People, is an advantageous Acquisition to this Kingdom, for they were not all poor as is well known at the Exchequer, and Royal Exchange, especially. if we give any credit to the Computation that has been made in *France*, of what they brought over, and of the loss that Kingdom has sustain'd. 'Tis confidently reported there, that sometime before the Revocation of the Edict of *Nantes*, and during the great Persecution, many Protestants foreseeing the Misfortunes likely to befall 'em, sent away a great part of their Estate out of *France*, insomuch that it's computed, the Refugees, one

with another, either in Money,
Goods, Jewels or other movables,
have brought over at least the value
of one Hundred Pounds Sterling,
whereby that Nation is so much im-
poverish'd in its Funds, (which it
has so much wanted since) to this
they add; that of necessary Consumption which is reckoned at 7 l.
Sterling *per* Head *per Annum ;* and
therefore by the Rule of contraries,
that Country whither they have
transplanted themselves, is by so
much the gainer. However 'tis hop'd
none will be so uncharitable as to
doubt, that out of Gratitude as well
as Affection, the Refugees are intirely devoted to the Nation that has receiv'd 'em with so much Humanity.
This will appear if it be consider'd
how great a share they had in the
Reduction of *Ireland,* where upwards
of 7000 of them perish'd either by
Sword or Sickness, which must
otherwise have fallen upon the English ; Some of the Refugees have endeavoured to subsist both by liberal

and mechanic Arts, and Husbandry,
but above all by their mutual Trade
and Correspondence with their Ac-
quaintance and Friends that have
settled in others Countries, as in
*Switzerland, Geneva, Germany, Hol-
land* and the Northern Crowns,
which has much increas'd all the
Revenues of this Kingdom, and
given a greater blow to *France*, than
six Civil Wars could other ways have
done, and at the same time have procur'd to this Kingdom in particular,
A real and lasting advantage, as the
House of Lords, was pleased to take
notice in a Conference with the Commons, about the Bill for preventing
Occasional Conformity, in
**Printed
in February
1703.* the words following page
(24) * *As to the Foreign Protestants, there is great reason to
give them all just encouragement, for as they
have brought among us many New Manufactures, so they have carried them so far,
that of late years we have exported to the
value of a Million of Woollen Manufactures, more than was done in King Charles's*

Reign, before they came among us ; and the putting them under Apprehensions or Discouragements, may be a means to drive them to a Country where they are sure of an intire Liberty. The Lords add, *We have felt the happy effects of the liberty granted them in the last Reign, and it is to be hoped, that nothing will be done in this to impeach that, or to raise Apprehensions and Fears in the minds of Men, that are so useful to us in the most important Article of our Trade.*

The opinion of that Noble House, who have thus eminently stood up for the Refugees, ought one would think to have silenced that multitude of malicious Libels that are daily Publish'd against 'em, whose Authors have so little modesty as to affirm, that the French are come over for want of means of subsistance, and not out of Zeal for Religion ; which Calumny the English Tradesmen magnify exceedingly because they say, that the French Refugees work cheaper than they do. Now supposing

that were true; it can be no damage
in the least, even to them that complain; For if a Shoemaker, for example, get 3 or 4 Pence less in a Pair
of Shoes, he on the other hand will
save that in his Gloves, and much
more in his Hat, which by the same
reason will be render'd as cheap in
proportion, and so of all other things.
But if any one would contest this
matter farther, we shall leave their
justification to the Landlords of those
Houses that have been built since
their coming over, the Rent of which
by a modest Computation cannot
amount to less than 80,000l. yearly,
and they without doubt will affirm
that their Refugee Tenants are no
ways prejudicial to the Nation, for
those of 'em that subsist of themselves, relieve to the utmost of their
Power such of their Brethren as are
necessitous, and readily pay both
Parish and National Taxes; They
have most of them been Naturaliz'd,
tho' at their own proper Charges, and
pay the Rent of their Churches, and

the Salaries of their Ministers, Readers and Schoolmasters, whereas in
other Countries, especially in *Holland*, the Refugees are naturaliz'd
gratis, they have the Freedom of
keeping Shops, and exercising their
respective Callings, and have been
supplied with above 100 Churches,
either in the United Provinces, or in
Germany, at the charge of the States
General, who very far from suffering
'em to pay the Ministers of the
Country, where they reside, do themselves pay the stipends of the Refugee Ministers, Readers and Schoolmasters, which are very considerable.
But what is yet more to their advantage is, that since the Persecution
which hath lasted now above 21
Years, most of which time the States
General have in Conjunction with
this Kingdom, being engaged in an
Expensive War against *France ;* not
one Refugee in *Holland* has ever
pay'd one Farthing for his Personal
Estate or Stock in Trade. One
might enlarge very much on this sub-

ject, were it not fear'd that the Libellers would insinuate from hence,
as tho' the Refugees complained,
whereas they are so far from it, that
'tis unwillingly they are forc'd to in-
stance in these things, to defend
themselves against those that endeavor to asperse them, with the taking away the Bread out of English-
men's Mouths, in order to render
them odious to the common People;
'Tis also in that view alone the Refugees alledge the advantagious settlement of their Brethren in *Branden-
bourgh*, the History whereof has been
printed at *Berlin*, by *Robert Roger*,
in 1690, which shews they believe in
that Country that the Refugees are a
very great Benefit to them, seeing his
Prussian Majesty is not content only
to favour them in his own Dominions, but likewise causes his Ambas-
sadors in other Protestant Courts to
make * Collects in the behalf of all
such Protestants as take Refuge in
his Countries.

* *Her Majesty's Brief for the Protestants of the Principality of Orange, Owned Subjects of his Prussian Majesty,
Dated the 17 November, 1703.*

If therefore all Politicians agree, that multitudes of People make the Glory of Kings, and the Riches of a country, why are then so many Libels suffer'd here to be Publish'd in opposition to those General Maxims? The Refugees think themselves under an obligation to declare it, and let the Publick know, that this Evil proceeds from the Enemies of their Religion; some unquestionable Proofs whereof shall be brought hereafter: But first 'tis proper to give an Account of a very remarkable thing that happened in the Year 1664. Some Popish Villages of the *District of Lalew* in the Low Countries Corresponding with *Amsterdam*, and coming accidently by some Books of Controversy, were soon perswaded of the Falsehood of the Popish Religion, and thereupon forsook it, which the Curates perceiving made their complaints to the Bishop, and the Bishop to the French King, after several Citations, Sentence was pronounced, that they should either go to Mass, or leave the Country, those Pious Christians rather chose the latter; at which King *Charles* II. was pleas'd to order Deputies to be sent thither to invite them over into *England*, and to make 'em very advantageous offers, besides the defraying their Charges; But the Kings of *Sweden* and *Denmark*, the States of *Holland*, and the Electors *Palatine, Saxony* and *Brandenbourg*, having at the same time sent their Deputies, the Conditions offer'd on the part of the Elector * *Palatine* being more advantageous than others, they Settled in his Country to the number of 1800 Men, Women, and Children, Tradesmen and Husbandmen, destitute of everything. But by reason of the late Wars in the *Palatinate*, and the destruction of *Billingheim*, they were obliged to leave that Country and settle in *Pomerania*, where they now are. This may serve to confute the

*Privileges granted to the Exiles of Lalew, in 17 Articles by Charles Lewis Earl Palatine, 5 August 1664.

unthinking Libellers; for no sufficient reason can be given why such
numbers of Protestants as come over
of themselves should be less esteem'd
than those who are invited by great
Offers. For they as well as these
encrease the Consumption of our
Manufactures and Products, especially that of Corn, and thereby save
the Five Shillings *per* Quarter on
what they consume, which would
otherwise be paid on Exportation;
Add to this the Sentiments of Sr.
Thomas Culpeper in his Political
Treatise, Sr. *William Petty* in his
Political Arithmetic, Sr. *Josiah Child*
in his new discourse of Trade, and
Sr. *Francis Brewster* in his Essays
on Trade, wherein its manifest all
their efforts chiefly aim at inculcating
the absolute necessity of an increase
of People, which they say is the
Source of Riches, and confess that
this Nation being under-peopled
stands in need of being Recruited.

It has already been said that the
Refugees to testify their Acknow-

ledgements have readily exposed
themselves to the perils of War, and
that in the Reduction of *Ireland*
above 7000 of 'em have perished;
which must once more be repeated,
because 'tis the sad Spring from
whence proceeds the great number
of Sick and Maimed Persons, Widows, and Orphans, that have lost
their Husbands, Fathers, Brothers
and other Relations, who during their
Lives supplied their Wants, besides
several Old Gentlemen, Old Ministers, and their Wives, who in Process
of time being grown weak and out of
employment, after having spent all
they had saved out of *France*, are reduc'd to the necessity of begging the
Public Charity of the Nation, and because 'tis these that are the most expos'd to the continual Machinations
of their Enemies, let this Preface inform the Reader of what perhaps he
may be unacquainted with, which is
the manner of their subsistance; since
a more favorable opportunity will
hardly ever offer it self, than the pres-

ent Publication of their Complaints against their Country-men. And to this purpose 'tis necessary to remind him of what pass'd in the Sessions of Parliament in 1695, when those Poor People presented a petition to the House of Commons, whereupon a Committee was appointed, in which upon the examination of their several Qualities, Ages and Callings; 'twas found that the number of Old Gentlemen, and Ministers, their Wives, Children, Widows and Orphans, was then 2460 Persons worthy of the Public Charity of the Nation, as appears by the Committee's Report to the House, containing the Declarations of King Charles the II. of the 28th of *July* 1681, and of King *William* and Queen *Mary* of the 25th of April 1689. mentioned in the said Report, importing, *That the French Protestants having been invited with great promises of assistance, to come hither, it were a great scandal to the Government and Religion, if they were not speedily relieved, and that it would be strange if this Nation should suffer itself to be outdone by their Neighbours in so excellent a work, seeing, that what Charity soever is bestow'd upon them* (besides the Blessing that redounds from it) *the Nation is ne'er the Poorer since it receives it back by Consumption as fast as it is given.* In consideration of which Report the House of Commons Voted 15000l. Sterling *per Annum* for the subsistance of those Poor Refugees. But 3000l. being appointed for the Ministers out of the said sum, there remain'd but 12000l. for the Laity, both here and in *Ireland*, which being then Paid in Remote Taillys and Malt Tickets, and the same being ordered to be Sold by the Lords appointed for regulating the Manner of distributing the Charity of the Nation. There was in 1696, 1697, and 1698, lost by them 6559l. 9s. 10d. which deprived the Poor of Seven Months Subsistance, during which time they were obliged to Borrow, what they could without having any prospect of repaying the same, unless

the Deficiency upon the Tallies should
be made good, which as it was never
done, has increas'd their Number.
This is the Account of what pass'd in
Parliament, one might add to the
Misfortune of that Deficiency, a yet
heavier loss for the Poor French Refugees, which is that they did not receive the Charity of the Nation, the
Year King *William* died, which was
then due and never paid, (the Warrant
for which is yet unsatisfied;) Which
losses inevitably oblig'd 'em to con-
tract Debts for their daily Sustenance,
which being wholly unable to satisfy
their Creditors, many of them have
acted rigourously to the utter ruin of
such as were left destitute by these
unexpected Deficiencies, which together with the Continuation of the
War, and the Calamities that attend
it have so increas'd their Misery, that
by a List newly Publish'd by Order
of His Grace the Lord Archbishop of
Canterbury, and the Lord Bishop of
London, containing the Quality, Age,
Sex and Habitation of every one, it

appears that from the Year 1696, and the Report then made to this present time, they are increas'd to more than double the Number, and that for some Years the 12000l. has not been sufficient to pay the rent of their Lodgings, and besides most of them being Old and Sick, let any one imagine the straights these Poor People are reduc'd to, (which is not fit to be Publish'd) and what Assistance can they expect from the other Refugees, who according to the Enemies Computation, have so little for themselves as will hardly suffice to maintain them; so that unless some more effectual means be found out for their Support, their Numbers without a miracle must daily increase; for humanly speaking, tho' the Refugees should exceed the * *Macedonians* in Charity to one another, nothing is to be expected but an addition of Misery. But there is reason to expect better things from this Charitable Nation, when with their wonted Compassion, they will be

* 2 *Cor.* 8. 2, 3.

pleased to take notice of the great occasion there is of exercising their Clemency towards such a number of miserable Objects, it being to be hop'd there are many who will follow the example of the Right Honorable Mr. Secretary *Harley*, whose Kindnesses and Charitable Offices proceeding from meer motives of Religion and Humanity towards these Poor Sufferers, they have often felt the good effects of, as well as of so many other Worthy Members of Parliament, who know, *That giving to the Poor is lending unto the Lord.**

It has already been observ'd that the Enemies of the Reformed Religion are those Libellers who are always endeavoring to propagate that of *Rome*, and strive to render the condition of the French Protestants bitter and grievous, they have Emissaries who make it their Business to descend from the general, even to the particular Persons of the Poor, whom they attack with grievous Calumnies, Reproaching them with having left

* Proverbs, *chapter* 19, *verse* 17.

their Wooden Shoes, and the Garlick and Onions they lived upon, to come hither to live at ease, and rob *Greenwich* Hospital, and the Widows, and Orphans of the Nation, of the Charities which they so much better deserve, and are now bereft of, by their being bestowed on such unworthy People. Thus they endeavor to deprive them of all manner of comfort, that they may be obliged to return to *France*, whilst on the other hand they make the Ways and means of repairing thither, very easy to such as are willing to go. Several instances of such Intrigues might be brought whereby they have enticed away many Children, who in *France* are put in Possession of the whole Estate of the Family, provided they abjure their Religion. Those Emissaries of *Rome* pretend to do those Evils that Good may come of it, but that is to accumulate Crime upon Crime, one of their Creatures had the Confidence to present a Petition to Her Majesty, and to his Grace the Lord Arch-

bishop of *Canterbury*, and the Lord
Bishop of *London*, importing that
the French Committee appointed by
the Lords Commissioners for distributing the Public Charity, were
false to their Trust, beseeching Her
Majesty to give him leave to secure
their Persons, and that in the mean-
time the Charity of the Nation should
be suspended; Upon this and such
like Representations Her Majesty
was pleased to order Sr. *Owen Buck-
ingham* the then Lord Mayor to
Summon the English Committee to
Examine the Matter, and make their
Report. The Person thereupon ap-
pearing before them could not make
out the least appearance of Misde-
meanor in the French Committee,
and finding that the * Report would
not be in his favour, and that Her
Majesty had order'd the Attorney
General to prosecute him, he made
his escape beyond Sea, since which
it was discover'd that he was a Papist
in disguise, that fled from *Piedmont*
for having killed a Priest; and his

* Report made the 26th July, 1705.

wife confess'd that he was to receive a Reward, could he have compass'd the Design of annulling the French Committee, which consist of Persons beyond all Suspicion, who give an exact Account of their Administration to the English Commissioners, who both the one and the other employ their Time, Care and Pains from no other Principle than their Duty to God and Charity to their poor Brethren, and yet such Representations, false as they are, having pass'd for current without any defence from afflicted Innocence, have proved of dangerous Consequence; for it hath been observed for some Years past, that the Charitable Example of several Worthy Christians, who have formerly left Gifts and Legacies at their Death, is very little followed at this time when there is so great an occasion for it, the Disuse of which Laudable Custom is in a great measure attributed to the subtle and crafty Insinuations of the Emissaries of *France* and *Rome*, who leave no means unattempted for the Destruction of the Refugees, whilst the Popish Tenet of the Merit of Good Works by the Pope's Indulgencies, and the Priests' Exhortations, is an almost incredible Support to the necessitous English and Irish Papists in *France*.

To sum up all from what has been said, 'tis to be hop'd no one will suffer himself any longer to be prejudiced against the Poor Refugees; But that all will submit to the favourable Declarations of those August Bodies the Houses of Lords and Commons, that so the great number of poor Members of Jesus Christ, who have escaped the Persecution and now implore the Charity of the Nation in a manner proportionable to their Wants, should live comfortably and Die in Peace, which might be effected, could it be contrived that each of Her Majesty's Subjects in *England* should give but a Penny every Year towards their Relief, (and that would suffice them,) which would not in the least be felt, if it be considered that it would all be spent here; besides as most of them are old and sickly, Death, humanly speaking, will in a very little time rid the Nation of them, and the Younger of them, who do not remember *France*, but with Sentiments of Resentment, are dayly blended among the English; Insomuch, that after the present War is ended, there should be liberty of returning, there are few will go back, but those that now seem to be chargeable to the Nation, and have left great Estates there, but their Number will be compensated doubly by the Parents and Friends of those that shall remain, who will be induced to come hither, where joyning with those whose Abilities and Talents permit 'em to enjoy the Happiness and Liberty they find, under the Reign of Her most Sacred Majesty, will altogether esteem it their Glory and Felicity to live here, and be faithful and zealous Subjects of the Country that has been their Sanctuary, and thereby encrease the Power and Glory and Riches thereof.

A
SHORT ACCOUNT

Of the COMPLAINTS,

A N D

Cruel PERSECUTIONS

O F   T H E

PROTESTANTS

I N   T H E

KINGDOM of FRANCE.

The Barbarities committed of late against the Protestants of *France*,, must appear so detestable to all who have not quite divested themselves of Humanity, and are such terrible Prodigies of Fury and Iniquity, as 'tis not to be wonder'd they who have

been the Authors thereof, should use
all sort of means to extenuate as
much as they can and to their utmost
endeavours keep from the knowledge
of the Publick the down right Truth
of the matter. Did we not know
that this was a project, which they
for a great while together, had concerted, and plotted, and into which
after long Deliberation they had pur-
posely introduced all those Injust
Passions, which have therein appeared in all their Colours, we might
possibly then say, that this their ex-
tenuation might be a mark of the
tacit condemnation of what they had
done, and suppose this their palliat-
ing an acknowledgment of their own
Displeasure at it.

But when Men Act in cold Blood,
and with a premeditated fury, how
extravagant soever their Actions are, it
is not usual for them to repent of 'em,
'tis therefore better to say, that if
this be not an effect of some remains
of shame, and remorse of Conscience,
we may suppose at least 'tis out of

some respect and regard to the
World, which do's not permit 'em to
expose to its View, those violences in
their true and natural Form, but on
the contrary obliges them to disguise
'em in order to diminish their horrour.

But whatever fine gloss may be set
on these Proceedings, it must be
however confessed, that it is an un-
conceivable Impudence thus to pretend to impose on the whole World
in matters of fact, so certain and so
publick as those are, and to endeavour
to put a cheat upon all Europe, as to
Transactions known, not barely by
Gazettes, or by Publick Prints, but
which is much more authentick, by
an almost infinite Number of the
very Persons themselves of all Ranks,
who are escaped, to set before the
Eyes of the remotest Nations their
Miseries and Calamities : Nay, it cannot be denied, but that after having so terribly overwhelm'd Innocent
People in their own Country, it is
beyond Barbarity it self, to endeavour
to stifle their Complaints in other

Countries whither they are driven. And by this means deprive them of a Compassion which even the bare Instincts of Nature, never refuse to the miserable. However, this is the course our Persecutors in *France* hold at this Day. Cruelty by their Order marcheth first, and then Imposture followeth after; That so all the Mischief which Cruelty hath brought forth, Imposture at the Heels of it may not only cover over, but likewise aggravate; to the end that the objects of their Fury may be left destitute of every Remedy, or Relief, be it never so small.

It were not reasonable to suffer them to go on, in this *Second* design, as they have done in the *First;* and therefore, till a more exact Account may be given of all the Particulars transacted in the different Acts of this Trajedy, we shall choose some principal Instances upon which we shall make such Reflections, as will enable the World to pass an equitable and impartial Judgment on the

whole Proceeding.   And as we shall
say nothing as to matters of fact, but
what is certainly and notoriously
known; So we shall advance nothing
in our Reflections, but what all, even
of the meanest Capacity, may easily
comprehend.

To begin with matters of fact;
there is no Body but knows, that a
little after his present Majesty of
France came to the Crown, there
arose in the Kingdom a Civil War,
which proved so sharp and desperate,
as brought the State within a Hair's
breadth of utter Ruin.   'Tis also well
known, that in the midst of all these
Troubles, those of the Reformed Religion still kept their Loyalty so inviolable, and accompanied it with
such a Zeal, and with a fervour so
extraordinary, and so successful, that
the King found himself oblig'd to
give Publick Marks of it, by a Declaration made at St. *Germains*, in the
Year 1652.   Then as well at Court
as in the Armies, each strove to pro-
claim loudest the Merits of the Reformed, and even the Queen Mother

herself was the first who set the Example, readily acknowledging, that they had indeed preserv'd the State. This is known by all; but 'twill hardly be believed, though it be too true, what our very Enemies themselves have an Hundred times told us; and which the sequel has but too shrewdly confirmed, that this was precisely the principal and most essential Cause of our Ruin, and of all the Mischiefs which we have since suffer'd; For endeavours were used to envenom all these important Services in the King's and his Ministers' minds, by perswading them, that if on this Occasion this Party could preserve the State, this sheweth they could likewise have overthrown it, had they ranked themselves on the other side? and might still easily do it if such a like Occasion should again offer itself. That therefore this party must by all means be crush'd, and the good they have done utterly disregarded, and look't on only, as an Indication of the Evil

which they may one Day be capable
of doing.

Now, that this way of reasoning
which refines upon all that is most
malicious and Diabolical, and proceeds, even so far as to hinder the
Subjects from discharging their Duty
to their Sovereign for fear of drawing
on themselves thereby Punishments
instead of the Recompenses which
they might reasonably expect, should
be relished as a piece of most excellent Policy, is that, which we could
never have thought, had we not been
convinced by experience; For as
soon as the Kingdom was settl'd in
Peace, the design of destroying the
Reformed was resolv'd on, and the
better to make 'em comprehend that
their Loyalty had ruin'd them, those
Cities which had shewed most of it,
were first begun with. Immediately
then, on slight pretenses, they fell
furiously on *Rochel, Montaubau,* and
Millau, these three towns, where
those of the Reformed Religion had
most signalized themselves for the
Interests of the Court; *Rochel* under-

went an incredible number of Pro-
scriptions, *Montaubau* and *Millau*
were sack'd by the Soldiers.

But these being but particular
stroaks and meer Preludes as it were,
which decided nothing; They tarried
not long before they made appear
the great and general Machines, they
were to use in the carrying on of
their intended design to the last extremity. It would be too difficult a
matter to give an exact Account of all
these several Methods and Engines,
the number of them was so prodig-
iously multiplied: For never did Hu-
mane Malice before produce such a
Fertil Crop of them, every Day bringing forth new ones for Twenty Years
together, and the Fund thereof all the
while never exhausted. To take only
notice therefore of the Chief of them,
and such as were most obvious to every
Eye; they may be reduced to these
Six Orders. 1. Those which relate
to the vexatious Suits and Trials in
the ordinary course of Judicature. 2.
Those which concern the Deprivation

from all kinds of Offices and Employments, and from all other ways of
Subsistance. 3. The Infractions of
the Edict of *Nantes*, under the Notion
and Title of Explications. 4. New
Laws and new Regulations. 5.
Juggling contrivances and tricking
Amusements. 6. And lastly, those
which had for their end the animating
of People, and inspiring them with
hatred and animosity against us.
These are the most considerable
means which the Persecutors have
employed to attain their Ends, and
the Paths which they have chosen to
tread in for several Years ; *I say for
several Years.* for what they had in
Prospect being no easy matter, they
needed therefore time to order their
Engines, and dispose their Materials;
not to take notice of their Traverses
also, and Interruptions by some
Foreign Wars, whose success did not
a little contribute to blow up their
courage, and to confirm them in
the design which they had formed
against us.

* *First Method of Persecution.*

*The First of these Means has had an almost infinite extent, as would easily appear if we should make a recital of all the Condemnations of Churches, or Suppressions of the Exercises of Religion, with all the other Vexations which have been brought about by the establishing of Commissioners of both Religions.

This Appointment of Commissioners out of both the Religions was a Snare the most Dextrously contriv'd that could be, for, immediately after the *Pirenean* Treaty, the King under pretense of redressing the Contraventions against the Edict of *Nantes*, establish'd them in the several Provinces. The Roman Catholic Commissioner was every where his Majesty's Intendant; who was to be sure a fit Man for the purpose, arm'd with all the regal Authority, and well instructed in the Secret. The other, was either some hungry Officer a Pensioner to the Court, or at best some Poor Gentleman, who had usu-

ally neither the Understanding requi-
site in these sorts of Affairs, nor the
Liberty of Speaking his Mind.   The
Clergy who had set them up, were
the Spring that made them move or
lie still at pleasure. The Syndicks
were received before them as formal
Parties in all our Affairs ; the Assign-
ations were given in their Name, the
Persecutions also, and as well the
Judgments of the Commissioners
when they were divided, as the Appeals from their Ordinances, were fi-
nally to be decided in the King's
Council.

Thus in general all the Priviledges
of the Churches, as well with Relation
to the Exercise of Religion, the
places of Publick Worship, and the
Rights of Burial, as all other depend-
encies were called in Question, and
consequently exposed to the fresh
Pursuits of the Clergy, and the ill Intention of the Judges.   In which
there was not the least spark of
Equity, for the Edict having been
once executed, according to the In-

tention of him that gave it, there
needed no second touches; it being
moreover wholly unlikely those of the
Reformed Religion, who had been
ever in the Kingdom the suffering
Party, could usurp anything therein,
and extend its Limits beyond what
belonged to them. But the providing
against the Contraventions was the
least of their Intention; and therefore by this Order, the greatest part
of the Churches, cited for the Justify-
ing of their Rights, saw themselves
soon condemned one after another,
by Decrees of Council, how good and
sufficient soever their Titles and De-
fences were. Scarcely passed there
a Week, wherein these kind of Decrees were not made; and if it so
happen'd that at any time the Judges
for very shame, saved any of them,
through the great Evidence of their
Right, as this sometimes happened;
besides that the number was small in
comparison of those that were condemned, the Judges often received express Orders to pass Sentence against

them, when they declared they could not do it with a safe conscience.

But the Oppressions of this kind did not terminate in the bare Condemnation of Churches; for particular Persons bore likewise their part. In ordinary and Civil Affairs, where the Matter was concerning, *Meum* and *Tuum* as perhaps a piece of Land, an House or a Debt between a Roman Catholick and a person of the Reformed Religion, Religion was always one of the chief Heads of the Accusation. The Monks, the Missionaries, the Confessors, and all the whole tribe of that Crew, interested themselves in the Affair. And in Courts of Justice all the cry was; *I Plead against an Heritick, I have to do with a Man of a Religion odious to the State, and which the King is resolved to extirpate.*

By this means, there was very little Justice to be expected, few Judges were proof against this false Zeal, for fear of drawing the Fury of the whole Cabal against them, or passing for favourers of Heriticks. 'Tis not to be imagined how many unjust Sentences these sorts of Prejudices have procur'd, in all the Courts of the Kingdom; and how many families have been ruined by 'em. And whenever any one complained, the Answer was ready. *You have the Remedy in your own Hands; why do you not turn Catholick?*

Yet all this had been nothing had the Persecution stopp'd here, and not proceeded to fasten on the Reputation, the Liberty, and even the very Lives of Persons, by a general Inundation (as, one may term it,) of criminal Processes and oppressive Trials. Orders were Printed at *Paris*, and sent from thence to all Cities and Parishes of the Kingdom, which impowered the Parochial Priests, Church-wardens and others, to make an exact inquiry into whatsoever any of the pretended Reformed might have done or said for Twenty Years past, as well on the subject of Religion, as otherwise, to make Informa-

tion of this before the Justices of the
Place, and Punish them to the utmost extremity.   Thence have we
seen for several Years in execution
of these Orders, the Prisons and
Dungeons every where fill'd with
these kind of Criminals.   Neither
were false Witnesses lacking; But
that which was most detestable was,
that though the Judges were sufficiently convinced they were Knights of the
Post, yet they maintained them, and
carry'd them through such Points, as
they knew to be palpably false.

Upon the Testimony of such Witnesses, and these too sufficiently
known to be so, they frequently
condemn'd the most Innocent and
Worthiest Persons to be whipt, to the
Galleys, to Banishment, and *Amende
Honourable.*   And if ever any Spark
either of Honor or Conscience did at
any time herein stop their hand, there
was always however a full Impunity
for those false Witnesses.

This kind of Persecution fell chiefly
on the Ministers; for of a long time
they might not Preach, without hav-

ing for Auditors, or to speak better Observators, a Troop of Priests, Monks, and Missionaries, and such kind of People, who made no scruple to charge them with Words, which they not so much as thought of; and to turn others into a quite contrary meaning. They also went so far as to divine the very Thoughts, that so they might charge them with Crimes; for as soon as ever any Minister spake but of *Egypt*, of *Pharaoh*, of the *Israelites*, of the *Godly* or the *Wicked* (as it was difficult not ·to speak of these Matters, when they explained the Scripture) those Spies never failed to report, that by *Egypt*, and by the *Wicked*, they meant the *Catholicks*, by *Pharaoh*, the *King*, by the *Israelites* the *pretended Reformed*. The Judges seemed to believe it, and fell in with it, and what is yet most surprising, the Ministers of State themselves respected these presumptive Interpretations, as so many evident Proofs. On these grounds, the Magistrates filled the Prisons with these poor People, keeping them therein for whole Years together and often inflicted on them also several corporal Punishments.

*'Tis already seen by this first kind of Perse- *Second Method of Persecution.* cution, what were the Usages in *France* towards the Reformed before they came to the utmost Violence. But we shall see them appear more evidently, in what we have to add, touching the Privation of Offices and Employs, and in general of the means of gaining their Livelihood; which is the second Way we mentioned, that has been used to effect their Ruine. 'Tis not hard to comprehend, that in a great Kingdom as *France* is, where the Protestants were dispersed, over all Parts, there was a vast Number, who could not subsist or maintain their Families, but by the Privilege of serving the Publick, either in Offices, Arts, Trades, or Faculties, each according to his respective Calling. *Henry* the Great was so well convinc'd of the Necessity and Justice of this, that he made it an express Arti-

cle, the most distinct perhaps and formal, of any contained in his Edict. And therefore in this Point the Persecutors the most exerted themselves, and stuck at nothing to compass their End.

'Twas in this View they began with the Freedom of Companies and handicraft Trades; which under several pretences, they rendered almost inaccessible to the Protestants, by the Difficulties of arriving to the Livery and Mastership of them, and by the excessive Expences, they must be at to be received into 'em; There being no Candidate, but was forced, for this purpose to be at the charge of tedious and expensive Law-Suits; under the Weight of which they were most commonly crushed. But this not sufficing by a Declaration made in 1669, they were reduced to one third, in the Towns where the Protestants were more in number than the other Inhabitants; and Orders were given not to receive any therein, till such Diminution was made: which at one Stroak excluded all the Pretenders.

Some time after they absolutely drove all the reformed from the Consulships, and all other municipal Offices of the Cities which was in effect, to deprive them of the Cognisance of their own Affairs. and Interests, wholy to invest the Catholicks with it.

In 1680, the King issued out an Order, which deprived them in general, of all kind of Offices and Employs, from the greatest to the smallest in his Farms and Revenues; they were made incapable so much as to exercise any Employ in the Custom-Houses, Guards, Treasury, or Post-Office, or even to be Messengers, Stage Coach Men, or Waggoners, or anything of this Nature.

In the year 1681, by a Decree of Council, all Notaries, Attorneys, Solicitors, Pursuivants, and Sergeants, making Profession of the reformed Religion were turned out and incapacitated throughout all the Kingdom.

The next Year they turned out of Place all the Officers who were Protestants belonging to the Nobility and Gentry, particularly to the Judges: strictly prohibiting at the same time any of the said Lords and Gentlemen to employ them in their Service, or even so much as to call them in to assist them in difficult Cases, as Assessors, or to give them simply their Opinions in Matters of Law and Right, and this upon no other Account but that of their Religion.

In 1683, All Officers belonging to the King's Household, and those of the Princes of the Blood; were also rendred uncapable of holding their Places, notwithstanding they were by Patent. The Counsellors and other Officers of the Court of *Ayds*, and Chambers of Accounts, and those of Seneshalships, Presidial Courts, Bayliwicks, and Royalties; Those also of the Admiralties, Provostships, and Marshalseas, with the Treasurers, Receivers and others who belonged to the Toll-Offices, and the publick Revenues, were ordered to quit their Places in Favour of the Roman Catholicks.

In 1684, all Secretaries belonging to the King, or the great Officers of the *Household* or *Crown* of *France*, as well Titular as Honorary, and their Widows were by an Act of Revocation deprived of all their Privileges of what Nature soever they were. They also deprived all those that had purchased any Privileges for exercising of any Profession, as Merchants, Surgeons, Apothecaries, Vintners, and all others, without exception.

Nay, they proceeded to this Excess, that they would not suffer any Midwives of the Reformed Religion to do their Office, and expressly ordained that for the future, our Wives should not receive Assistance in Child-birth from any but Roman Catholicks.

'Tis not to be exprest how many particular Persons, and Families they reduced every where, by these strange and unheard of Methods, to Ruine and Beggary. But because there were yet many who could sustain themselves other Methods of Oppression must be invented. To this Purpose they issued out an Edict from the Council, by which, the new *Converts*, as they call them, were discharged from any Payment of Debts, for three Years. This, for the most part, fell on the reformed, who, having had a more particular Tye of Interest and Affairs with these pretended Converts because of their Communion in Religion, were reckon'd among their chief Creditors. By this Invention they had found the Secret to recompense those that changed at the expense of those that did not; and this they did likewise by another Decree; for they discharged the new *Converts* of all the Debts which those of the Protestant Religion had contracted in common; which by consequence fell on the others.

Add to this, the Prohibition to sell or alienate their Estates, on any Pretence whatsoever, the King annulling and breaking all Contracts, and other Acts relating to that Matter, if it did not appear, that after these Acts, they had stayed in the Kingdom a whole Year: so that the last Remedy of helping themselves

by disposing of their Estates in extream Necessity, was taken from
them. They deprived them likewise
of another which seemed the only one
remaining, which was, that of seeking
their Bread elsewhere, by retiring into
foreign Countries, there to get their
Living by Labour, since this was not
permitted them in *France;* by repeated Edicts the King forbad them to
leave his Kingdom, on severe Penalties, which drove them to the last Despair, since they saw themselves reduced to the horrible Necessity of
Dying with Hunger in their own
Country, without daring to go to
live elsewhere. But the cruelty of
their Enemies stopt not here, for there
yet remained some Gleanings in the
Provinces, though very few, and as
thin as those in *Pharaoh's* Dream.
The Intendants in their Districts
had Order to Load the Reformed
with Taxes ; which they did, either
by laying upon them the Tax of the
New Catholicks, who were discharged
thereof in favour of their Conversion,
or by laying Arbitrary Taxes, which

were called *Taxes of Offices*. That is to say, he who in the Ordinary Roll was assessed at Forty or Fifty Livres, was charged by this exhorbitant Imposition at Seven or Eight Hundred. Thus had they nothing more left, for all was a Prey to the Rigour of the Intendants. They exacted the Payment of those Taxes by Quartering of *Dragoons*, or Rigourous Imprisonment; from whence they were not freed till they had pay'd the utmost Farthing.

These were the Two First Machines which the Clergy made use of against us: To which they added a * Third, which we ** Third Method of Persecution.* have termed the Infraction of the *Edict* of *Nantes*, under pretence of Explication. Those who would know their Number and Quality, need only Read the Books Written and Publish'd on this subject, as well by the Jesuit *Meynier*, an Author, famous for his Cavilings, as by one *Fillau* of *Poitiers*, and *Bernard*, an Officer in the Presidial Court of *Besiers* in *Langue-*

doc. There you will find all the Turns, which the meanest and most unworthy Sophistry, could invent to elude the clearest Texts of the Edict, and to corrupt the sincerity thereof. But because we here give you only, a brief Abstract of our Troubles, and the Molestation we met with, we will content ourselves, with observing some few of the principal only, issuing from this Fontain.

What was there, for Example, more clear and unquestionable in the Edict than this, *viz.* That 'twas given with an intention to maintain those of the Reformed Religion, in all the Rights that Nature and Civil Society have endued Mankind withal? To argue thereupon would be but meer Trifling, and yet under pretence that the Edict contained not in Express Words, that the Natural Children should be left under the Tuition of their Fathers and Mothers to be brought up by them in their own Religion; the King without any regard, that this is one of the first and most Inviolable Rights of human Nature, and as if the Edict aforesaid had made no Provision thereupon, by a Declaration of *January* 1682. Ordained that all Natural Children of either Sex, and of what Age and Condition soever, should be Instructed and Educated in the *Roman* Catholick Religion. It is very important in this place to take notice of the Words, *of what Age soever they be*, For that gave Birth to a World of Persecution, since the Adversaries were not content to use this Order with restriction to the time to come, but all Natural Children were enquired after. Among whom were some of at least Four score Years of Age, that had passed all their Life in the Protestant Religion, who by virtue of this Order were Imprison'd and grievously Oppress'd uppon the supposition that they were obliged to be Catholicks by their birth.

Nor must it be omitted that in the Year 1683, there came out an Edict, that Children might at the Age of Seven Years, Abjure the Reformed

Religion, and Embrace the Catholick under pretence, that the Edict did not precisely mention, that at this Age they should continue at their Parents Disposal.　Who sees not that this was a meer Fetch, seeing that on one Hand, the Edict positively Prohibited to take away Children from their Parents by force, or persuation, by which it was undoubtedly meant till Age of Discretion or Maturity should Emancipate them; And on the other hand it suppos'd, and confirm'd all the *Natural* Rights, of which without Controversie, this is one of the most inviolable.

Was there ever also a more manifest Infraction of the Edict, than that, which forbad those of the Protestant Religion, who had passed over to the *Roman*, to return to that they had left, under pretext, that the Edict did not formally give them in express terms this liberty? For when the Edict permits to all the Kings Subjects in general Liberty of Conscience, and forbids the perplexing or troubling them, or offering any Force, contrary to this Liberty; Who sees not, that this Exception touching the pretended Relapsers, is so far from being an Explication of the Edict, that 'tis indeed a notable Violation of it?

Where-unto we may add the Prohibition to the *Roman* Catholicks not to change their Religion, and embrace the Reformed. For when the Edict gives Liberty of Conscience, it does it in proper Terms. For *all those who are, and shall be, of the said Religion.* Yet if we believe the Clergy, this was not *Henry* the Great's meaning, who according to them must have intended only to grant it to those, who made Profession of it, at the time of the making his Edict.

The Edict of Nantes gave also to the Reformed, the Privileges of keeping small Schools in all places where they had the Exercise of their Religion, and by this Term of *small or little Schools*, according to the common explication, those were always Understood where one might Teach Latin

and Humanities.   This is the Sense
which has been ever given all over
the Kingdom, to this expression; and
which is still given when it concerns
Roman Catholicks, yet by a new sort
of Interpretation, this Permission was
restrained to the bare Liberty of
Teaching to Read, and Write, and
cast Accounts, as if the Reformed
were unworthy of Learning anything
further, and this on purpose to tire
out the Parents, and drive them to
this extremity, either not to know
how to Breed up their Children, or
else be forced to send them to the
Roman Catholicks for Education.

The Edict gave them Power
in all Places where they had
Churches, to instruct publickly
their Children, and others, *in all
what concerns Religion*, which visibly establish'd the Right of teaching
Theology; seeing their Theology is
nothing else but their Religion, and
as to Colleges, wherein they might
be instructed in Philosophy and other
liberal Sciences, which is properly

called a College, the Edict promis'd
Letters Patent in good form. Yet
'twas interpreted that the Edict gave
no Right to the Reformed to instruct
them in Divinity, nor to have Colleges; and on this supposition it was,
that Three Universities were condemned, which were all that remained,
viz. Saumur, *Puilaurans*, and *Die :*
That of *Sedan*, although founded on
a particular Edict, was supprest as
well as the rest, and even before them.

But amongst all the Infractions of
the Edict of this sort, there has been
none more solemn or more daring
than the annulling or abolishing of
the Courts of Justice, which had been
granted by *Henry the Great* as a perpetual Establishment, with an equal
number of Judges of both Religions,
for administring Justice without Prejudice or Partiality, and for causing
his Edict to be religiously observ'd.
Nevertheless under Pretence that it
was said that the Two Courts established at *Castres* and *Bourdeaux*
might be incorporated with their

Parliaments, when the Reasons that had moved his Majesty to have them separated, should cease. The present King by his Edict supprest also those of *Paris* and *Rouen*, and then by another soon after those of *Grenoble, Toulouse*, and *Bourdeaux*. Leaving by this means his Protestant Subjects expos'd to the Rage and Injustice both of the Parliaments, and other inferiour Courts, insomuch that it is not to be conceived what Vexations they have hence endured both as to their publick and private Concerns.

But we must go further, and seeing we have undertaken to shew in this Abridgment, the principal things they have done to exercise our Patience, before they came to the utmost Fury: We are not to pass over the new Orders, * or new Laws, which were as many new Inventions to torment us. The first of these Orders which appear'd was touching the manner of Burials and Interring

* The Fourth Method of Persecution.

the Dead. The Number of Attend-
ants were reduc'd to *Thirty* Persons,
in those Places where the Exercise
of our Religion was actually Established, and to *Ten* where it was not.
And the like Regulations as to Number were afterwards made as to most
other occasions which we might
have for meeting together about
our Affairs.

Orders were also issued out to
hinder the Communications of Provinces one with another, by Circular
Letters or otherwise, though about
Matters of Alms, and Disposal of
Charity, Prohibitions were likewise
made of holding Colloquies in the
interval of Synods ; excepting in two
Cases, the Providing for Churches
destitute by the decease of their
Ministers, and for the Correction of
certain Scandals. They likewise
took away from those Places allowed
by the Edict, which they call'd *Exercises in Fief*, all the Marks of
Public Religious Exercise, as the
Bell, the Pulpit, and other things of

this nature.   They were likewise forbidden to receive those Ministers in Synods to Vote, or to Register them in the Catalogue of those that belong to Churches.

The Ministers in general were forbidden to take on them the Title of Pastors, or any other, beside that of Minister of the Pretended Reformed Religion.   Others forbad the Singing of Psalms in Private Houses ; Some too commanded them to cease Singing, even in their Churches when the Sacrament pass'd by, or at the time of any Procession.   Others were made to hinder Marriages, at such times as were forbidden by the Church of *Rome.*   Others forbad Ministers to preach anywhere, except in the place of their usual Residence. Others forbad their setling in Places unless sent by the *Synods*, though the Consistories should call them hither in due form.   Others were made to hinder the Synods from sending to any Churches more Ministers, than were there in the preceeding Synod.

Others to hinder those that design'd for the Ministry, to be Educated in Foreign Universities. Others Banisht all Foreign Ministers, though they had been Ordained in the Kingdom, and spent there the greatest part of their Lives. Others forbad Ministers, or Candidates for the Ministry, to reside in Places where Preaching was forbidden, or nearer than Six Leagues of the same. Others forbad the People to Assemble in the Churches, under pretence of Praying, Reading or Singing of Psalms, except in the presence of a Minister appointed by the Synod. One ridiculous one was made to take away all the Backs of the Seats in the Churches, so to reduce them all to an exact Uniformity. Another, to hinder the Churches that were somewhat Richer, to assist the Weaker either towards the Maintenance of their Ministers, or other Necessities.

Another was made to oblige Parents to give their Children, who should change their Religion, great

Pensions. Another to forbid Marriage betwixt Parties of different Religions, even in the case of scandalous Cohabitation. Another to Prohibit those of the Reformed Religion, from that time, to entertain in their Houses any Domesticks, or Servants, that were *Roman* Catholicks. Another which made them uncapable of being Named Trustees or Guardians. And consequently put all the Minors, whose Fathers Dyed in the Profession of the Protestant Religion, under the Power and Education of *Roman* Catholicks. Another forbidding Ministers and Elders to hinder any of their Flocks, either directly or indirectly from embracing the *Roman* Religion, or to disswade them from it. Another forbidding *Jews* and *Mohametans* to embrace the Reformed Religion, and the Ministers either to Instruct, or receive them into it. Another subjecting Synods to receive such *Roman Catholick Commissioners* as should be sent them from the King, with an express

Order to do nothing but in their
Presence. Another forbidding the
Consistories to assemble oftener than
once a Fortnight, and then always in
the presence of a Catholick Commissioner. Another forbidding the Consistories to assist, on pretence of
Charity the poor Sick Persons of
their Religion; and ordaining that
the sick should be carried into the
Hospitals, strictly forbidding any
Man to entertain them in their
Houses. Another Confiscating in
favour of the Hospitals, all the Lands,
Rents, and other Profits of what nature soever, which might any Wise
have appertained to any of the condemned Churches. And another forbidding Ministers to come nearer
than Three Leagues to the Place
where the Privileges of Preaching
were in question or so much as con-
tested. Another Confiscated to the
use of the Hospitals all the Revenues, and Rents, set apart for the
Maintenance of the Poor, even in
such Places where the Churches were

yet standing.   Another subjecting
Sick and Dying Persons to the necessity of receiving Visits from Judges, Commissaries, or Church-Wardens; as well, as from Parish Priests,
or their Curates, Monks, Missionaries, or other Ecclesiastics; thereby
to induce them to change their Religion, or require of them express Declarations concerning it.   Another forbidding Parents to send their Children
under Sixteen Years of Age to Trav-
el in Foreign Countries on any Pretence whatever.   Another prohibiting
Lords and Gentlemen to continue the
Publick Exercise of Religion in their
Families without first producing their
Titles before the Commissioners, and
obtaining their License for the same.
Another which restrained the Right
of Entertaining a Minister to those
only, who were in possession of their
Lands, even since the Edict of Nantes, in a direct or collateral Line.
Another which forbad the *Bailywick*
Churches to receive into them any of
another *Bailywick*.   Another which

enjoined Phisicians, Apothecaries, and Chirurgions, to advertise the Parish Priests, or Magistrates, of the condition of Sick *Protestants* that they might visit them.

But amongst all these new Laws, those which have most served the Design and Intention of the Clergy have been, on one Hand, such, as Prohibited the receiving into their Assemblies any of those who had changed their Religion, or their Children, or any *Roman Catholick* of what Age, Sex or Condition soever, under pain of forfeiting their Churches, and the Ministers doing *Amende Honourable*, with Banishment and Confiscation of their Estates; and on the other hand such, as that which enjoined the setting up in all the Protestant Churches a particular Bench for the Catholicks to sit on; For by this means, as soon as any one, but resolved to change his Religion, there needed no more but to make him do it in private, and then to find him next morning in the Church, there to be observed by the

Catholicks, who were in their seat;
Upon which immediately Informations were constantly made, and Condemnations procured according to all
the Rigour of the Law.   The *Roman
Catholicks* needed only to come into
the Church under pretence they had
a place there, and then they slipt in
amongst the Crowd, and immediately
this was a Contravention, to the Declaration, and was followed by an un-
avoidable Condemnation.   'Tis by
this means they have destroyed an incredible number of Churches, and
put into Irons a great many Innocent
Ministers, for Villains and False Witnesses were never wanting on those
occasions.

     * All those Proceed-
ings were so violent,   *Fifth Method
that they could not but   of Persecution.*
make a strange impression on the
Minds of the Reformed; And indeed
a very little stock of Penetration was
sufficient to discern the Drift and
Design of such ways.   And in effect
there were many of them that opened

their Eyes and bethought themselves
seriously of their safety, by leaving
the Kingdom; transporting themselves some into one Kingdom, and
some into another, according as their
several Inclinations led them. But
this was what the Court no wise intended, for more than one reason;
and therefore to hinder them, they
renewed from time to time, the Decrees we have mentioned, which
strictly Prohibited, under the most
severe Penalties, any to depart the
Realm without Leave; And to this
End they strictly guarded all Passages on the Frontiers. But all these
Precautions did not Answer their
Expectations; And 'twas thought
worth their while to Blind the People,
by hopes of abating this rigourous
usage at Home, and hiding from 'em
the mighty Design they had in View;
And to that End in 1669, the King
was persuaded to Revoke several Violent Decrees, formerly given in Council, which produced the desired effect.
For though the Judicious saw well

enough that this Moderation sprang
not from a Right Principle; and that,
in the Sequel, the Former Decrees
were put in Execution; yet the most
part imagined they would still Confine
themselves within some Bounds, and
not pass to a total destruction of us.

We have often Drawn the same
Conclusions from the several *Verbal*
Declarations, which came many times
from the King's own Mouth, as that
he pretended not to indulge us, but
would do us perfect Justice, and permit us to enjoy the Benefits of the
Edicts in their full Extent.   And
that although he should be very glad
to see all his Subjects Re-united to
the Catholick Religion, and would
for the effecting thereof contribute all
his Power, there should yet be no
Blood shed during his Reign, nor any
Violence exercis'd on this account.
These precise and often reiterated
Declarations, gave us hopes the
King would not forget them;
and that especially in *Essential*
Matters he would suffer us to en-

joy the effects of his Equity.
This we were the more induced to
believe from a Letter he Wrote to His
Electoral Highness of *Brandenbourg*,
the Copies of which the Ministers of
State took care to Disperse through
the whole Kingdom. Wherein his Majesty assured him, that he was so well
satisfied with the Behavior of his *Protestant* Subjects, and that having engaged his Royal Word to maintain
them in their Rights and Privileges,
his Intention was to let them enjoy
the same, from whence we Drew this
Natural Conclusion; that he intended
not utterly to Extirpate us at that time.

To which we may add the Manage-
ments sometimes used in the Council,
where some Churches were preserved,
at the same time others were ordered
to be demolished, to make the World
believe, they observed some measures
of Justice; and that those which they
condemned, were consequently not
grounded on good Titles. Some
times they softened several too rigourous Decretal Orders of the Provin-

cial Parliaments; Other times they
seemed not to approve of the Violences offered by the Intendants and inferiour Magistrates, so far as even to
give Orders to moderate or suspend
them. And accordingly they hindered the execution of a certain Decree
made in the Parliament of *Rouen*,
which enjoined those of the Reformed
Religion to kneel when they met the
Host. Thus did they stop too; the
Persecutions of a Puny Judge at
Charanton, who ordered us to strike
out of our Liturgy a Prayer composed
for the Faithful, that groaned under
the *Tyranny of* Antichrist. 'Tis thus
also, that they did not extreamly favour another Persecution, which began to be general in the Kingdom
against the Ministers, under pretence
of obliging 'em to take an Oath of
Allegiance, wherein other Clauses
were incerted, contrary to what Ministers owe to their Charges and Religion. 'Twas thus likewise they
suspended the execution of some
Edicts, which themselves had made,

as well to compel the Ministers to pay taxes as to oblige them to reside constantly in the Place where they ex- ercis'd their Function.   With the same design the Syndicks of the Clergy, had the Art to let the princi- pal Churches of the Kingdom alone for many Years, without disturbing their Assemblies ; whilst in the mean time they took away all those in the Country.   They suspended also the condemnation of the Universities, and reserved 'em for the last.   It was also in this view that at Court, they seemed at first not able to believe, and at last not to ap- prove, of the excesses, which were committed in *Poitou* by one *Maril- lac*, an Intendant of that Province, a Man both cruel and greedy to the highest degree; and fitter much to be sent in the Highway, than to be made Intendant of a Province; though indeed he was let loose, on purpose for these Exploits.

But amongst all these tricking ways, there are none more remarkable, than Five or Six, which it will not be improper here to relate. The *First* was, That at the very time, when at the Court they issued out all the Decrees, Declarations, and Edicts, which we have before spoken of, and which they caused to be put in Execution with the greatest Rigour; Nay while they Interdicted the Churches, Demolish'd the Temples, deprived Particular Persons of their Offices and Employments, reduced People to Poverty and Hunger, Imprison'd 'em, Loaded 'em with Fines, Banish'd 'em, and in a word, ravaged almost all; yet at the same time the Intendants, Governours, Magistrates, and other Officers in *Paris*, and over all the Kingdom, cooly and gravely gave out that the King had not the least intention to touch the Edict of *Nantes*, but would still most Religiously observe it. The *Second* was, that in the same Edict, which the King publish'd to forbid *Roman Catholicks* to embrace the Reformed Religion, which was in the Year 1682. (That is to say, at a time when they had already greatly advanced the Work of our Destruction,) they caused a formal Clause to be inserted in these express Terms, *That he confirmed the Edict of Nantes, as much as it was, or should be needful.* The *Third* was, that in the Circular Letters which the King wrote to the Bishops and Intendants, to oblige them to signifie the Pastoral Admonitions of the Clergy, to our Consistories, he tells them in so many words. *That his Intention was not that they should do anything that might attempt, upon what had been granted to those of the Pretended Reformed Religion, by the Edicts and Declarations made in their favour.* The *Fourth*, that by an express Declaration published about the latter End of the Year 1685, the King commanded that the Ministers should not reside in the same Church, above the space of Three Years, nor return to the first within the space of *Twelve;* and that they should be thus Translated from Church to Church,

at least Twenty Leagues distant from
one another; supposing by a manifest Consequence that his Design was
yet to permit the Exercise of Religion, to the Ministers in the Kingdom
for *Twelve Years at least.* Tho' indeed they had at that Moment design'd the Revocation of the Edict,
and had resolved it in the Council.
The *Fifth* consists in an Address
presented to the King, by the Assembly of the Clergy at the same time,
that an Edict to revoke that of *Nantes*, was drawing up, and actually put
into the hands of the Attorney General to model it; and in the Decree
which was granted on this address,
the Clergy complained of the Misrep-
resentations which the Ministers are
wont to make of the *Roman* Church,
to which they attribute, say they,
Doctrines which they do not hold,
and beseech'd his Majesty to provide
against it, expressly declaring that
they did not yet desire the *Revocation*
of the Edict, upon which the King by
his Decree peremptorily forbad the
Ministers to speak either good or bad

directly or indirectly, of the Church of *Rome* in their Sermons, from whence it was natural for every one to conclude 'twas his Intention they should still preach. Were ever such pitiful and treacherous Shifts seen! Or was there ever any greater than this which was put into the very Edict we are speaking of: The King after having cancell'd and annull'd the Edict of *Nantes*, and all that depended thereon; and having interdicted forever all publick religious Exercises, after having forever banish'd all the Ministers from his Kingdom, yet expressly declares, that his will is, that his other Subjects, who were not willing to change their Religion, might abide within the Realm in full Liberty, enjoy their Estates, and live with the same freedom as heretofore, without being at all molested on Account of their Religion; till it should please God to enlighten and convert them. These were Amusements and Snares to trapan the simple and unwary, as it has since appeared, and still does more and more every day by the horrible Usages they suffer, and of which we shall have occasion to speak hereafter.

* But we shall first mention another pre- *The Sixth Method of Persecution.* paratory Stroak which the Persecutors have not failed to make use of, which we have reckoned the sixth in order. It consists in disposing the People insensibly to desire our Destruction, to approve it when done, and to diminish in their Minds that Horror which they must naturally have had, at the Cruelties and Injustices of our Persecutors. For this purpose several Methods were used, and the commonest have been the Sermons of the Missionaries and other controversial Preachers, with which the Kingdom was for some Years stock'd under the Title of *Royal Missions.* It was ordinary to choose in *France* for this End the most virulent and hot-brain'd Zealots, who had such an Education given them, which far from making them moderate, rather enflamed them; so that 'tis easy to apprehend what Actors these were like to

be, when they not only found themselves upheld but saw themselves
moreover set on, and had express
Orders given them to inspire their
Hearers with Fury. And so well did
they acquit themselves in this matter,
that 'twas not their Fault if popular
Commotions did not follow in the
great Cities, even in *Paris* it self, had
not the prudence of the Magistrates
prevented them.

To the Preachers we must joyn the
Confessors and Directors of Conscience, the Monks, the Parish Priests,
and in general, all Ecclesiasticks from
the highest to the lowest; for as they
were not ignorant of the true Intention of the Court in this Affair, every
one would be striving who could
show most Zeal, and Aversion to the
Reformed Religion, because they all
found their Interest therein; this being the readiest Way to raise and establish their Fortunes. In this Design
of animating the People, there past
few Days wherein the Streets did not
ring, as well with the Publication of

Decrees, Edicts, and Declarations against the Protestants, as also with satyrical and seditious Libels, of which the People in the Towns of France are very greedy.

But these things served only for the meaner sort of People, and the Persecutors had the Mortification to see this their Design disapproved by all those who were one Degree above the Mob. Wherefore they imploy'd the pens of some of their Authors, who had already acquired some Reputation in the World; and amongst others that of the Author of the History of *Theodosius the Great*, and that of Mr. *Maimbourg*, heretofore a Jesuit. This last publish'd his History of Calvinism, which he has since had the leisure to repent of, by the smartest and weighty Answers which have been made to it. Their Example was followed by several others; and *Monsieur Arnaud* who loves always to make one in such Matters where he may vent his Spleen would not deny himself the satisfaction here, of pleasing his Humour; and at the same time of endeavouring to recover the Favour he had lost at Court. But altho his *Apology for the Catholicks*, was a work as full of Fire and Passion as the Bigots themselves could have wish'd, yet was it not relish'd because his Person was not; he was so ill gratified for it, that he complained thereof to the Archbishop of *Rheims* in a Letter, the Copies whereof were dispersed all over *Paris*, amongst other things he exaggerated his Misfortune and compared himself with another, who for much less Service had received from the King a Reward of Twenty Thousand Livres. This more and more expos'd the Character of the Person.

However they stood in no great need of him, as not wanting virulent Writers; amongst whom we must not forget one Souldier, formerly (as they say) a Tailor, and at present Author of the History of the *Edicts of Pacification;* nor Mr. *Nicole* once a great *Jansenist*, and now a Proselite of the Archbishop of *Paris;* Author of the Book entitled, *Protestants convinced of Schism.* Nor the Author of the *Journal des Savans,* who in his ordinary Diaries fiercely contends for the Catholick Faith's being planted by Fire and Sword: alledging for the proof thereof the example of a King of *Norway,* who converted the Nobles of his Country by threatning them to *slay their Children before their Eyes, if they would not consent to have them baptized and be baptized themselves.* And for a long while together we have seen in *Paris,* and elsewhere, nothing but such sort of writings: To such a Degree was their Passion heightened.

Whilst all these things, which we have observed, were transacting in *France,* and they by great steps advanced to their End;

* Tis not to be imagined that the Reformed neglected their common Interests, or did not all that became a just and lawful Defence. They frequently sent from

* The Methods taken by the Reformed for their Defence.

the remotest Provinces their Deputies to Court: They maintained their Rights before the Council; thither they brought their Complaints from all parts. They employed their Deputy General to solicit their Interests, as well with the Judges and Ministers of State, as with the King himself, some times also they presented general Addresses, in which they represented their Grievances with all the Humility and Deference that Subjects owe to their Sovereign. But they were so far in this from being heard, that their Troubles were continually increased: and so their second Estate became worse than the first. The last Petition presented to the King himself by the Deputy General in *March* 1684, was express'd in Terms the most submissive, and the most capable of moving Pity, as every one may judge, it having been since printed ; and yet it produced no other Effect but the hast'ning on of what had been long resolve'd upon, namely by open force to compass our Ruine.

* This was effectual-
ly brought about some
Months after, and ex-
ecuted in a manner so terrible and so
outragious, that, as we said in the
beginning, there are few in *Europe*,
how distant soever from the noise of
the Public Occurrences who have not
heard the Report of it; but 'tis certain the Circumstances are not Known
to all, and therefore we shall· give an
Account of them in few Words,
were it but to stop or silence the
Impudence of such who are not
ashamed to publish, that no Violences
have been committed in *France*, and
that all the Conversions there have
been made with free and full Consent.
They forthwith took the Method of
quartering Soldiers in all the Provinces almost at one and the same time,
which were chiefly Dragoons that are
generally the basest Troops of the
Kingdom, and Fellows that will stick
at nothing. Terror and Dread march-
ed before them: and, as it was
concerted, all *France* was in an instant filled with this News, that the

King would no longer suffer any *Huguenots* in his Kingdom; and that they must resolve to change their Religion, nothing being able to prevent it.

They began with the Province of Bearn, where the Dragoons did their first Executions, which were followed soon after in the *higher* and *lower Guienne, Xaintonge, Aunix, Poitou*, the *upper Languedoc, Vivarets*, and *Dauphine*, after which they came to the *Lioneois*, the *Cevennes*, the *lower Languedoc, Provence*, the *Vallees*, and the Country of *Gex;* afterwards they fell on the rest of the Kingdom, *Normandy, Burgundy*, the *Nivernois* and *Berry;* the Countries also of *Orleans, Touraine, Anjou, Britany, Champagne, Picardy*, and the *Isle of France*, even extending to *Paris* itself, which have all undergone the same Fate. The first thing the Intendants were order'd to do, was to summon the Cities and Commonalities. They assembled the Inhabitants thereof, who profest the reformed Religion, and told them, 'twas the King's Pleasure they should without Delay turn Catholicks, which if they would not do freely, they should be made to do it by force. The poor People, surprised with such a Declaration, made Answer, *They were ready to sacrifice their Estates and lives to the King, but their Consciences being God's they could not in that manner dispose of them.*

There needed no more to make them immediately bring the Dragoons, which were not far of, the Troops immediately seized on the Avenues and Gates of the Cities; they placed Guards in all the Passages, and often enter'd with Sword in Hand, crying, *Dye or be Catholicks:* They were Quartered at Discretion on the Reformed, with a strict charge, that none should depart out of their Houses, nor conceal any of their Goods or Effects on great Penalties; yea, even on the Catholicks, that they should either receive or assist 'em in any manner. They began with consuming all the Provisions the House afforded, and gutting them of all their Money,

Rings, and Jewels; and in fine, Bleeding them of whatsoever was most valuable. After this they distrained the Household Goods, inviting not only the Catholicks of the Place, but also those of the neighboring Cities and Towns to come and Buy the said Goods, and other things that would yield Money. Afterwards they fell on their Persons, and there was no wickedness, or Horror, which they did not put in Practise, to force them to change their Religion.

Amidst a Thousand hideous Lamentations and horrid Blasphemies, they hung Men and Women by the Hair of the Head, or the Feet to the Roofs of the Chamber, or to the Racks in the Chimneys, and there smoked 'em with whisps of wet Hay, till they were no longer able to bear it; and when they took 'em down, if they would not sign, they hung 'em up immediately again. They pluck'd off the Hair of their Heads and Beards, with Pincers, till they left none remaining. They threw them on great Fires kindled on purpose, and pull'd them not out til they were half Roasted. They ty'd Ropes under their Arms, and Plung'd them again and again in Wells from whence they would not take them up, till they had promised to renounce their Religion. They bound them as they do Criminals, put to the Question; and in this Posture with a Funnel they poured Wine down their throats, till the fumes of it depriving them of their Reason, they were made to say they would consent to be Catholicks. They stript them naked, and after having offered them a Thousand infamous Indignities, they stuck them with pins from top to bottom. They lanc'd them with Pen-knifes, and sometimes with red hot Pincers, took them by the Nose, and so dragged them about the Room till they promised to turn Catholicks, or till the Cries of those poor Wretches, that in this condition called on God for Assistance, constrained them to let 'em go. They Bastinadoed them most cruelly, and then dragg'd them thus Bruised to the Churches where this forced appearance of theirs was accounted an Abjuration; They kept them from Sleeping, Seven or Eight Days together, by relieving one another that they might Watch them Night and Day, and keep them still Waking: They some times threw Buckets of Water on their Faces; They tormented them a Thousand ways, and held over their Heads Kettles turned downwards, whereon they made a continual Dinn, till these poor Creatures had even lost their Senses. If at any time they found any Sick Persons, either Men or Women, that kept their Beds, with Feavers or other Diseases, they had the Cruelty to bring a number of Drums, to Beat an Alarm about them for whole weeks together, without any Intermission, till they should give their Word they would change. It has in some places happened, that they have tyed Fathers and Husbands to the Bed Posts, while before their Eyes they Ravished their Wives and Daughters without even being brought to condign Punishment for it. They pluckt off the Nails from the Hands and Toes of some, which was not to be endured without intolerable Torment. They Blew both Men and Women up with Bellows even till they were ready to burst.

If after these horrid usages, there were yet any that refused to turn, they Imprisoned them; and for this chose Dungeons the most Dark and Noysom, in which they exercised on them all sorts of inhumanity. In the mean time they demolished their Houses, desolated their Lands, cut down their Woods, and seized their Wives and Children to Imprison them in Monasteries. When the Soldiers had devour'd and consumed all that was in an House, the Royal Farmers furnished them with subsistence, and to reimburse themselves, Sold by Authority of Justice the Estates of such Gentlemen, and put themselves in Possession thereof. If some to secure their Consciences, and escape the Tyranny of these Merciless Men, endeavoured to save themselves by Flight, they were pursued and hunted in the Fields and Woods and shot at like Wild Beasts. In order to which the Provosts Patrolled upon the High Ways, and the Magistrates of Towns had orders to stop all them without exception, and bringing them back to the Places from whence they fled, they used them like Prisoners of War.

But we must not fancy that this Storm fell only on the common sort, Noblemen and Gentlemen of the best Quality were not exempted from it. They had Soldiers Quartered upon them in the same manner, and were treated with the same fury as Citizens and Peasants were. They plundered their Houses, wasted their Goods, rased their Castles, cut down their Woods, forced away their Children, and their very persons were exposed to the Insolence and Barbarity of the Dragoons, no less than others. They spared neither Sex, Age, nor Quality, where ever they found any unwillingness to obey the Command of chang-

ing their Religion, they practised the
same Violences. There were still remaining some Officers belonging to
the Parliaments, who underwent the
same Fate, after having been first deprived of their Offices; nay even the
Military Officers, who were actually
in Service, were ordered to quit their
Post and Quarters, and repair immediately to their Houses there to suffer the like storm ; if to avoid it, they
would not become Catholicks. Many
Gentlemen and other Persons of
Quality, and many Ladies of great
Age, and of Ancient Families, seeing all these Outrages, hoped to find
some Retreat in *Paris*, or *at Court;*
Never imagining the Dragoons would
come to seek them out so near the
King's Presence. But this hope was
no less vain than all the rest, for immediately there was a Decree of Council, which commanded them to leave
Paris and *the Court* within few
Days, and to return without delay to
their own Houses with a Prohibition
to all Persons to entertain or Lodge

them in their Houses. Some having attempted to petition the King, complaining of these cruel Usages and humbly beseeching his Majesty to stop the Course of them, could obtain no other Answer, but that of being sent to the *Bastille* where they suffered the same Persecutions.

Six Remarks. Before we proceed any further, 'twill not be amiss to make here some *remarks;* the first shall be, that almost every where, at the Head of these infernal Legions, besides the Commanders and Military Officers, the *Intendants* and *Bishops* march'd every one in his Province or Diocese, with a Troop of Missionaries, Monks, and other Ecclesiasticks.

The Intendants gave such Orders as they thought most effectual to carry on Conversions; and to restrain natural Pity and Compassion; if at any time it should find (which was not often) a Place in the Hearts of the Dragoons or of their Commanders. And as for my Lords

Bishops, they were there to keep
open House, to receive Abjurations,
and to have a general and severe
Inspection, that every Thing might
pass according to the Intentions
of the Clergy.   The Missionaries
and Ecclesiasticks were there to
animate the Soldiers to such an
Execution so agreeable to the
Church, and so glorious to God and
his Majesty.

The second Thing observable is,
that when the Dragoons had made
any yield, by all the Horrors which
they practiced, they immediately
changed their Quarters, and sent
them to those who still persever'd.
This Order was strictly observ'd
in this Manner, even to the End,
insomuch that those who persever'd
to the last, and had shewn the
greatest Constancy, had at last the
whole Number of the Dragoons,
which at the beginning were dispers'd amongst all the Inhabitants
equally, quarter'd upon them alone,
which was indeed a Load impossible
to be born.

A third Remark, which we shall make, is, that in almost all the considerable Cities and Towns, they took care before they sent Troops thither, to gain by means of the Intendants or some other underhand Way, a certain Number of Persons not only to change their Religion themselves, when it should be required; but also to assist in perverting others. So that when the Dragoons had sufficiently play'd their Part, the Intendants with the Bishop, and the Commander of the Forces, would again assemble these miserable Inhabitants, that were now utterly ruin'd to exhort them to obey the King, and become Catholicks; adding withal the most terrible Threats that could be to over-awe them; and then those they had before gain'd never fail'd to execute what they had preingag'd, which they did with the more Success inasmuch as the People did as yet, put some kind of Confidence in them.

A fourth Observation is, that when

the Master of the House thinking to
get rid of the Dragoons, had obey'd
and sign'd what they would, he was
not freed for all this, if his Wife,
Children, or the meanest of his Domesticks did not do the same; and if
his Wife, or any of his Children, or
Family fled, they ceas'd not torment-
ing him, till he had made them return: which often times being impossible, the change of his Religion did
not at all avail him.

The fifth is, that when these poor
Wretches fancied their Consciences
might be at rest, by signing some
Form of an equivocal Abjuration,
which was so tender'd on purpose, to
ensnare them, these Villains would
in some short time after come to
them again, and make them Sign one
sufficiently strong and binding, which
drove them into the utmost Despair.
Nay farther, they had the Baseness
to make 'em declare, that they embraced the Romish Religion of their
own full and free Consent without
having been won to it by any indirect

or violent means. If after this they
scrupl'd to go to Mass, or did not
communicate, if they did not assist
at Processions, or omitted going to
Confession, if they did not tell over
their beads, or if a Sigh slip'd from
them, signifying their unwillingness
they had immediately Fines laid on
'em and were forc'd to receive again
their old Guests the *Dragoons*.

The sixth and last remark is. As
fast as the Troops ravaged in this
manner the Provinces, spreading Terror and Desolation in all Parts, Orders were sent to all the Frontiers and
Seaport Towns, strictly to guard the
Passes, and stop all such as pretended
to escape out of the Kingdom; so that
there was hardly any Hope for these
poor Wretches, to save themselves by
Flight. None being permitted to pass
without having a certificate, either
from his Bishop, or Curate, that he
was a Catholick, those who had not
were put in Prison, and used like
Traytors. As for any Permission
freely to depart, 'twas in vain to at-

tempt it. That was constantly deni'd;
And all foreign Vessels lying in the
several Ports were narrowly searched;
the Coasts, Bridges, Passages to Riv-
ers, and the High-ways were all carefully guarded, both Night and Day.
And the Persecution was carry'd to
that height, that some of the neighbouring States were requir'd not to
harbour any more Refugees, and even
to send back such as they had already
received. Attempts were also made
to seize on, and carry away some, who
had escaped into foreign Countries.

Whilst all this was now acting in
the Kingdom, the Court was no less
busy in consulting to give the finishing
* Stroak; which con-
The Revocation sisted in rigging out an
of the Edict Edict to repeal that of
of Nantes. *Nantes.* Much Time
was spent in drawing it up, both for
Matter and Form, for some would
have the King detain all the Ministers, and force them as well as the
Laity to change their Religion, or
else condemn them to perpetual Im-

prisonment. They alledged, that if that were not done, they would be as so many dangerous and inveterate Enemies against him, in foreign Nations. But others on the contrary affirm'd, that as long as the Ministers continued in *France*, their presence would encourage the People to persevere to the utmost in their Religion, whatsoever Care might be taken to hinder it; and that supposing they should change, they would be but as so many secret Adversaries, sheltered within the Bosom of the Romish Church, so much the more dangerous as their Knowledge and Experience in controversial Matters was great. This last Reasoning prevailed, and so the resolution was taken to banish the Ministers, and to allow them no longer time than fifteen Days to depart the Kingdom. And then the Draught thereof was deliver'd to the Attorney General, of the Parliament of *Paris* to draw it up in such Form, as he should judge most fitting. But before the publishing of it, two Things were thought necessary to be done;

the first was to oblige the Assembly
of the Clergy at their breaking up, to
present to the King the above mention'd Address, in which they told
his Majesty, they desired not for the
present the repealing the Edict of
Nantes.   And the other was to issue
out an Order of Council to suppress
all kind of Books made by those
of the reformed Religion, by the first
of these, the Clergy thought to shelter themselves from the Reproaches,
which might be cast on them as the
Authors of so many Miseries, Calamities, and Oppressions, as this Repeal
would inevitably occasion,   And by
the other they pretended to make the
Conversions, (as they styled them,)
much more easy, and confirm those
which had already been made, by taking from the People all Books, which
might either instruct, fortifie, or bring
them back again.

  To conclude, this Revocative Edict
of *Nantes*, was seal'd and publish'd
on *Thursday*, the 18 of *Oct*. in the
year 1685.   The Court being then at
Fontainbleau, 'Tis said Mounsieur

Letelier the then Chancellor of *France* shew'd an extream Joy at the sealing it; but that lasted not long, this being the last time of his holding the Seals, for as soon as he return'd from *Fontainbleau*, he fell immediately sick, and died within a few Days; leaving both the reformed and others matter for Reflection on the Fate of the Persecutors, into the Number of whom his Politicks rather than his natural Inclination had forc'd him in his latter Days.

This Edict was registerd in the Parliament of *Paris* on *Monday* the 22th following in the Vacation contrary to all Form. And presently after it was passed in like manner in the other Parliaments.

It contains in it, a Preamble and twelve Articles. In the Preamble the King shews how neither *Henry the Great* his Grandfather, did give the Edict, nor *Lewis* the XIII his father confirm it, by his other Edict of *Nimes*, but with a Design of endeavouring more effectually the Reunion of their

Subjects of the pretended reformed Religion, to the Catholick Church, and that this was also the very Design which he had himself at his first Accession to the Crown. That he had been hindered in this by the Wars, which he was forced to carry on against the Enemies of his Crown and State; but that at present being at Peace with all the Princes of *Europe,* he wholly gave himself to the bringing about this Reunion. That God had been graciously pleased to enable him to accomplish it, seeing the greatest and best Part of his Subjects of the said Religion had embraced the Catholick, these Edicts of *Nantes* and *Nimes* with others were consequently become void and useless.

By the *first Article* he therefore suppresses and repeals them in all their Extent; and ordains that all the *Protestant Churches* yet standing in the Kingdom of *France* and in all the Countries, Territories, and Lordships under his Obedience should immediately be demolished. By the *Second* he forbids all Sorts of Assemblies for the Exercise of said Religion be they of what kind soever. The *Third* prohibits religious Exercise in the Families to all the Lords and Gentlemen of Quality, under penalty of corporal Punishment and Confiscation of their Estates. The *Fourth* banishes all the Ministers out of his Kingdom, and Territories thereto belonging, and enjoins them to depart thence within fifteen Days after the Publication of this Edict under Pain of being sent to the Gallies. By the *fifth* and *sixth* he promises Rewards and Advantages to the Ministers who should change their Religion, as also to their Widows after them. In the *seventh* and *eighth.* He forbids the instructing of Children in the pretended reformed Religion: and ordains that those who shall be born henceforward shall be baptiz'd, and educated, in the Catholick Religion; enjoining the Parents to send them for this End to the Churches, under the Penalty of being fined 500 Livres. The *ninth* gives four Months time to such Persons as have already departed the Kingdom to return; otherwise their Goods and Estates to be confiscated. The *tenth*, with repeated Prohibitions, forbids all his Subjects of the said Religion to depart out of his Realm, either they, their Wives or their Children, or to convey their Effects, under the Pain of the Gallies for the Men, and of Confiscation of Body and Goods for the Women. The *Eleventh*, confirms the Declarations heretofore made against those that relapse. The *Twelvth* declares, that as to the *rest* of his Subjects of the said Religion, they might till God enlighten them, remain in the Cities of his Kingdom, Countries, and Lands under his Obedience, and there continue their Commerce or Trade, and enjoy their Estates, without being troubled or molested upon Pretence of the said Religion; on Condition only that they hold no Assemblies under Pretext of praying or exercising publickly, any kind of Religious Worship.

* In Execution of this Edict, the very same day that it was registred and published at *Paris*, they began to demolish the Church of *Charenton*. The oldest Minister * thereof was commanded to leave *Paris* within four and twenty Hours, and forthwith to depart the Kingdom. For this end they put him into the Hands of one of the King's Footman, with orders not to leave him till he was out of his Dominions. His Colleagues were little better treated; they gave them forty-eight Hours to quit *Paris* and left them afterwards, to pursue their Journey upon their Parole. The rest of the Ministers were allow'd the fifteen days; but it can hardly be believed to what Vexations and Cruelties they were exposed. First of all, they neither permitted them to dispose of their Estates, nor to carry away any of their Moveables or Effects nay they disputed them their Books and private Papers, on Pretence, that they must

* Pastor Claude.

first justifie, that these their Books and
Papers did not belong to the Consistories wherein they serv'd which was
a Thing impossible, since there were
no Consistories then remaining. Besides they would not give 'em leave to
take along with 'em Father or Mother,
Brother or Sister, or any of their Kin-
dred; though there were many of them
infirm, decay'd and poor, which could
not subsist but by their Means.   They
went so far, as even to deny them their
own Children, if they were above
seven Years old; nay some they took
from them that were under that Age,
and even such as yet hang'd upon
their Mother's Breast; and refused
them Nurses for their new born In-
fants, which the Mothers could not
give suck to.

In some frontier Places they stopp'd
and imprison'd them, upon divers
ridiculous Pretences, sometimes alledging they must prove, that they
were really the same Persons which
their Certificates mentioned.   At
other times they wanted to be in-

form'd whether there were no criminal Process, or informations against
them, and sometimes again they would
force them to prove that they carried
away nothing that belonged to their
Flocks.   Then after they had thus
detained and amused 'em, they would
tell them that the Fifteen Days of the
Edict were expired, and they could
not longer have Liberty to retire, but
must be sent to the Gallies.   There
was no kind of Deceit or Treachery
which they did not make use of to
molest them.

As to the rest, whom the Force of
Persecution and hard Usage constrained to leave their Houses and
Estates, and to fly the Kingdom, 'tis
not to be imagined what Dangers
they exposed themselves to.   Never
were Orders more severe or more
strict, than those that were given
against them.   They doubled the
Guards in Sea-port Cities, High-ways
and Foards; They cover'd the Country with Souldiers; they armed even
the Peasants either to stop or kill those
that passed: They forbad all the Offi-

cers of the Customs to suffer any Goods, Moveables, Merchandize or other Effects to pass.   And in a word, they forgot nothing that might hinder the Flight of the persecuted even to the interrupting almost all Commerce with the neighbouring Nations.   By this means they quickly filled all the Prisons in the Kingdom ; for the Dread of the Dragoons, the Horror of seeing their Consciences forced, and their Children taken from them, and of living for the future in a Land where there was neither Justice nor Humanity *for them*, obliged every one to think of an Escape, and to abandon all to save their Persons. All these poor Prisoners have been since treated with unheard of Rigour, confined in Dungeons, loaded with heavy Chains, almost starved with Hunger; and deprived of all converse but that of their Persecutors.   They put many into Monasteries where they experienced some of the worst of Cruelties.   Some indeed have been so happy as to dye in the midst of their Torments, but others have at last sunk under the Weight of the Temptation; and some again by the extraordinary Assistance of God's Grace, do still sustain it with an Heroick Courage.

These have been the Consequences of this new Edict, but who would not have believed that the *Twelfth Article* would have sheltered the *rest* of the Reformed, that had a Mind still to tarry in the Kingdom; since this Article doth so expressly assure them, that they might live therein, continue their Trade, and enjoy their Estates without being at all troubled or molested upon pretence of their Religion. Yet behold what they have done, and still are doing to these poor Wretches, they did not recall the Dragoons and other Souldiers, which had been sent into the Provinces before the Edict: On the contrary they to this day commit with greater Fury, the same Inhumanities and Barbarities, which we have before represented; besides this, they have filled those Provinces since

with Souldiers where there were none
before, as *Normandy, Picardy, Berry,
Champagne,* the *Nivernois, Orleans,*
the *Blesois* and the *Isle of France.*
They exercise the same Violence, ex-
ert the same Fury there as they do in
other Provinces. *Paris* it self, where
methinks this Article of the Edict,
should have been best observ'd, because so near the King's Presence,
and more immediately under the Government of the Court, *Paris,* I say,
was no more spared than the rest of
the Kingdom. The very day the
Edict was published, without more
delay, the Attorney General and some
other Magistrates, began to send for
the Heads of Families to come to
them, they declar'd to 'em that 'twas
absolutely the King's Will they should
change their Religion; that they were
no better than the rest of his Subjects, and that if they would not do it
willingly, the King would make use of
those means which he had ready to
compell them to it. At the same time
they banish'd by Letters under the

privy Seal the Elders of the Consistory, together with some others in whom they found the most Constancy and Resolution; and the better to disperse them, chose out such Places as were most remote from Commerce, where they have ever since used them with a great deal of Cruelty, some have comply'd, but others are yet under Sufferings.

The Diligence of the Attorney General and Magistrates not succeeding so fully as they wish'd, though Threats and Menaces were not wanting; *Monsieur de Seignelay*, Secretary of State would also try what Influence he could have within his Jurisdiction at *Paris*, for this End he got together about an hundred or an hundred and Twenty Merchants and others into his Palace, and after having caused the Doors to be shut, he forthwith presented them with a certain Form of Abjuration, and commanded them in the King's Name presently to sign it; declaring that they should not stir, till they obeyed

The Contents of that Form were, not only that they did renounce the *Heresy of Calvin*, and enter into the Catholick Church, but also that they did this *voluntarily*, and without being forced or compelled to it. This was done in a most imperious manner, and with an haughty Air of Authority: there were that dar'd to open their Mouths, but they were sharply answered, that they were not to dispute but to obey; so that they all sign'd before they went out.

To these Methods they added others more terrible, as Prisons, the actual Seizure of their Effects and Papers, the taking away of their Children, the Separation of Husbands and Wives; and in fine, the hard Method, that is to say, *Dragoons*. Those that most firmly stood out, they sent to the *Bastille* and to the Fort *Leveque;* The Houses of as many as they could not find, or had hid themselves, were seal'd up, they plunder'd many others, not sparing their Persons, just as they had done in other Places.

Thus the *Twelfth* Article of the Edict, which promised some Relaxation, or Shadow of Liberty, was nothing but an egregious deceit to amuse the credulous, and keep them from thinking to make their escape, a Snare to catch them with the more ease.

Fury still kept on its usual course, and was heated to such a degree, as not content with the desolation committed in the Kingdom, it reached even into *Orange*, a Sovereign Principality, where the King of Right has no Power, and thence taking the Ministers away by force, transported them into his Prisons. Thither the Dragoons were likewise sent, where they executed all kind of Mischiefs and Villany, and by force constrained the Inhabitants thereof, both Men, Women and Children, nay, and the very Officers of the Prince, to change their Religion.

This was the state of things in the latter End of the Year 1685, and the full Accomplishment of the Threats the Clergy had made us three Years

before, towards the End of their Pretended Pastoral Letter, Ye must expect misery incomparably more dreadful and intolerable, than all those,
which hitherto your Revolt and your
Schism have Drawn upon you.   And
truly they have not been worse than
their Word, there are some notwithstanding in the Kingdom who still
abide firm; and their Persecutions
are still continued to them; New
Torments are daily invented against
those whom Force has made to
Change their Religion, because they
are still observed to Sigh and Groan
under their hard Bondage, their
Heart detesting what their Mouths
have Profest, or their Hands signed.
As to such as have escaped into
Foreign Countries, who are at least
*An Hundred and Fifty Thousand
Persons*, their Estates are Confiscated;
this being all the hurt they can do
to them at present.   I say *at present;*
for 'tis not question'd but our Persecutors are contriving to extend their
Cruelties further.   But we must hope

in God, that whatsoever intentions they may have of destroying the Protestant Religion in all Places, he will not permit them to effect their design. The World will surely open its Eyes; And this which they have now been doing with an high Hand, and worse than barbarous fury, will shew not only the Protestants, but the wise and sober Catholicks, what they are to expect both one and other, from such a sort of People.

* In effect, he that shall give himself, but the leisure to reflect on the matters of fact

* Reflexions upon all these Cruel Persecutions.

which we have just now related, the which are most evident, notorious, and acted in the face of the Sun, shall see not only the Protestants opprest, but the King's Honour sullied, his Countries damnified, all the Princes of *Europe* Interested; nay, even the Pope himself, with his whole Church and Clergy, shamefully discredited, and defamed.

*For to begin with the *King* himself. What   *First Reflection.* could be more contrary to his Dignity than to put him upon breaking his Word, and persuading him that he might lawfully and with a safe Conscience violate, by a Thousand Contraventions and Breaches, and at last utterly revoke and annul, so solemn an Edict as was that of *Nantes*.

That Edict which was granted by *Henry the Great* in the Year 1598, hath Four Incontestable Characters that are justified by the very Text it self. 1. That it was a Royal and Sovereign *Promise*, which he granted, not only for himself, and for the Term of his own Reign, but also for that of all his Descendants and Successors for ever. 2. That of being a Solemn, Definitive, and Irrevocable *Decree*, pronounced by the Sovereign Magistrate, to continue for ever, as a Regulation and Law between the two contending Parties, the *Roman Catholicks* and the Protestants, after both had been duly and sufficiently heard.

3. That of being a Treaty or Accord accepted, agreed upon, and consented to, by the whole Realm in Quality of a *perpetual* Law and Regulation. And 4. that of having been made sacred, and even divine, by the *reciprocal Oath* of the whole Nation.

I say, that these four Characters are incontestable, and to be justified from the very Text of the Edict. The first is evident from the Preamble, wherein the King, after having exhorted his Subjects rightly to understand that in the Observation of that Law did consist the chief Foundation of their Union, and Concord, Tranquility and Peace, and the Restoration of the State to its primitive Splendour, Wealth and Dignity, he adds, We on our Part promise to cause the same exactly to be observed, and not to suffer it to be any ways violated, and then to shew he meant that his promise should oblige his Posterity and Successors, he declares, he grants it *as an Edict perpetual and Irrevocable.* And having particularly express'd the Articles of it, he concludes, in these words, we declare expressly that our Will is that this our Edict be firmly and inviolably kept and observed by all our Justices, Officers, and all other our Subjects, and that no Respect or Regard shall be had to any thing that might be contradictory to or derogatory from the same.

And accordingly Lewis XIII. at his Accession to the Crown lookt upon it, as a Law to the Observation whereof he found himself engaged, acknowledging by his Declaration, that it was an Edict perpetual and irrevocable which stood in no need of being confirmed, the King now reigning has acknowledg'd the same upon several Occasions. This is then a Royal Word and Promise of *Henry the Great,* not only on behalf of himself, but also in behalf of his Posterity, and thence it follows ; that 'tis a Condition annex'd to his Inheritance and Crown never to be separated from it.

The second Character is no less certain and manifest than the first, it appears by the Preamble of the Edict wherein the King declares that he did not grant this Law, but till after he had on one Side consider'd the Representations of his Catholick Subjects, and on the other side permitted his Subjects of the pretended reformed Religion to meet by their Representatives, to draw up theirs, and to put together all their Remonstrances, and upon that Account conferr'd with them at several Times. Adding, that he judged it necessary to set forth at present, upon Consideration of the whole Matter to all his said Loving Subjects, a Law that might be universal, clear, plain, and absolute whereby they should regulate themselves upon all Differences, which formerly did, or hereafter might arise betwixt them. This then is a Judgement after a fair Hearing of both Sides, and a Regulation no less fit to adjust all former Differences, than to put an end to those that might happen thereafter: and consequently, *'tis a perpetual and irrevocable Edict*, as he terms it himself; not in a titular Way only, as Kings are sometimes wont to express themselves, but really and in its own Nature.   And accordingly he further declares he gives it, after having, with the Advice of the Princes of his Blood, the other Princes, the Crown Officers, and other Grandees and notable Members of his Council of State being near him, diligently weighed and considered the whole Matter.

As for the 3d Character there cannot be desir'd a better Proof than its having been registred in all the Courts of Parliament of the Realm, in the Chambers of Accounts, Courts of *Ayds*, *Baylewicks*, *Seneschalseas*, *Provostships*, and all other Jurisdictions whatsoever, according as it was order'd by the last Article thereof. The Parliament indeed of *Paris* and *Toulouse* a little scrupled it at first, but those Difficulties were soon over, and there was no Opposition either from the Clergy or from the Body of the Catholicks, on the contrary, the Promulgation of it was with the full Consent of the whole Realm, as even the aforementioned *Bernard* Counsellour of Beziers hath acknowledged in his pretended Explanation of the Edict of Nantes. After the publication of this Edict, says he, the King sent Commissioners into all the Provinces of the Kingdom to put it in Execution, and to re-establish his Religion where it had been disused, but we do not find by the verbal Relations of those Commissioners, that they did anything considerable, or that any Controversies were brought before them, concerning the Exercises of Religion, and other Important Matters, either because they were willing to prevent the reviving of the Differences already terminated, and the kindling a-new the Heats that were so lately appeas'd; or because the Exercise of the Catholick Religion having been interrupted a long while in many Places, they were content to have it everywhere restored.

As to the 4th Character one need only read the XCII Article, wherein the King ordains in express Terms, that the Observation of his Edict shall be sworn to by all the Governours and Lord Lieutenants of Provinces, Bailiffs, Seneschals, and other ordinary

Judges, by Mayors, Aldermen, Capi-
touls, Consuls, and Jurats or Sheriffs,
either Annual or by Patent for Life,
also by the Principal Inhabitants of
Cities and Towns, as well Catholicks
as Protestants, and lastly, by the
Courts of Parliament, Chambers of Accounts, and Court of Ayds. All which
was punctually executed accordingly.

Any the least of these Characters
were sufficient, one might think, tho'
separated from the rest, to put the
Edict out of the Reach of the Capriciousness and Fickleness of *such is our
Will and Pleasure*, for who can doubt
but that a King is oblig'd to keep his
Word, and his faith, and likewise that
of his Predecessors too; when the
same is become a condition insepara-
bly annexed to the Succession; as undoubtedly it is, if it has been granted
under the Quality of a Solemn, perpetual, and irrevocal Promise. It were
impertinent to say, that a King can't
oblige himself towards his own Subjects, or that it is inconsistent with his
soveraignty. For not to enter into the
Discussion of that Principle, which

would lead us too far, if examin'd with Application, I say, if the solemn Promises of Kings do not oblige them towards their Subjects, they at least are obligatory *to themselves*. A King sure is no better than God. Who though he be infinitely elevated above his Creature, all Divines nevertheless agree that his Promise binds him so far *to himself* that it is immutable, for which Reason the Scripture so often speaks of his *Fidelity* and *Veracity*, in the Performance of the Conditions contained in his Covenant with us. Who can doubt, but a King may bind himself to observe and cause inviolably to be observ'd the Laws which Justice has inclin'd him to grant his Subjects, for regulating their Differences by the Rules of Right Reason, and preserving them all from their mutual Oppressions? How much more then is he bound when his Subjects also on both Sides have agreed to it; and the Law made for both their mutual Benefits, is become *the publick Faith* of his whole Kingdom? And how much more yet when the Covenant, or Treaty

has been reciprocally and solemnly
sworn to, by a whole Nation, and
God himself become thereby the De-
pository and Avenger of it?   How
is it then possible that those evil Coun-
sellours should have perswaded the
King, to break through all the Bar-
riers of Justice, Fidelity, and Conscience;   and without any regard
either to God, the State, or himself, to
make his Power his only Rule.

To palliate in some sort the Violence of this Procedure they make
him say in this new Edict, that the
best and greatest Part of his Subjects,
of the Pretended reformed Religion
have embraced the Catholick; and
that therefore the Execution of the
Edict of Nantes, with whatsoever else
has been done in Favour of the same
Religion was become void.   But is not
this an Evasion unworthy of his Majesty, seeing that if this *best and great-*
est Part of his Subjects of the reformed Religion embraced the Catholick; 'tis certain they have been con-
strain'd to it by Force, and the cruel

and furious Oppression which his Troops have laid on them.

Perhaps this might indeed be said, had the *better* and *greater* Part of his Subjects chang'd their Religion of their own Accord, altho that in this Case too, the Privileges of the Edict must have continued for those that remain'd. But after having forc'd them to change by the horrible Inhumanities of his Dragoons, after having depriv'd them of the Liberty which the Edict gave 'em; to say coldly, that he only revokes the Edict, because it is now become *useless*, is a Raillery unbefitting so great a Monarch: for it is as much as if he said, that he was indeed oblig'd to continue to his Protestant Subjects all the Privileges due to them; but that having himself overthrown them by a *Major Force*, he finds himself at present lawfully and fairly disengag'd from his Obligation: which is just as if a Father, who himself had cut his childrens Throats, should glory in the being from that time forward freed from the Care of nourishing and protecting them.　Are Kings wont thus to express themselves in their Edicts?

What they make him further say, to wit, that *Henry the Great*, his Grandfather of glorious memory, granted the Edict of Nantes to those of the pretended reformed Religion only that he might the better effect their Reunion to the Roman Church; that Lewis XIII also his Father of glorious memory, had the same Design when he gave the Edict of Nimes; and that he himself too, had entred thereinto at his coming to the Crown; is but a pitiful Salvo, but taking it for granted since they will have it so, and let us state it nakedly and literally in the Sense they give it us in, what can we conclude thence, but these following Propositions?　(1)　That *Henry* the Great and Lewis the 13 granted those Edicts to our Forefathers only on Purpose to deceive them, and with an intent afterwards to ruine them with the greater Facility under the Mask of this Fraud.　(2)　That not being themselves able to effect this, being hindred by their other Affairs, they committed this most important Secret to his present Majesty, to the end he should execute it when he met with a fitting Opportunity. (3) That his present Majesty entring into the Thought of this, at his first coming to the Crown, he confirm'd those Edicts and set forth his Declarations of 1643 and 1652, with other Decrees advantageous to the Reformed Religion, only the more cunningly to impose on them, and lay Snares in their Way, or if you please, to crown them, as they crowned of old the Victims when they were to be sacrific'd. (4) That all that has been done against them since the Peace of the *Pirennees*, till this very time, according to the Abridgment which we have here made of it, has been only the Execution of a Project, yea even of a Project far more Ancient than we imagin'd, seeing we must date it from the time of the granting of the Edict of *Nantes* it self, and go back as far as to *Henry the Great* for it, and in fine, that that which has been till now a great and profound Mistery is no longer so; seeing the

King by this new Edict discovers it
to all the World, that he may be ap-
plauded for it.

Can any Body but confess, that if the
Enemies of *France* had undertaken
to discredit the Conduct of its Kings,
and render them odious to the World,
they could not have taken a more
successful Course. *Henry the Great*
gives his Edict to the Protestants
with the greatest Solemnity imaginable, he gives it to them as a Recom-
pence of their Services, he promises
solemnly to observe it; and as if this
was not enough, he binds it on the
whole Kingdom by an Oath : he exe-
cutes it to the utmost of his Power;
and they peaceably enjoy'd it to the
end of his Reign : yet all this is but a
meer Snare, for they are to be dra-
goon'd at a proper time : but being
himself surpriz'd by Death he could
not do it, but leaves it in Charge to
Lewis the XIII. his Son.

Lewis the XIII ascends the Throne,
issues out his Declaration immediately, that he acknowledges the Edict of

Nantes as perpetual and irrevocable, and such as needed not any new Confirmation, and that he would religiously observe every Article of it, and therefore sends Commissioners accordingly to see it actually put in Execution.   When he took up Arms he protested that he had no Design at Religion; and in Truth he permitted the full Liberty of it, even in those very Towns he took by Assault, he gives after this his Edict of *Nimes* as the Edict of a *Triumphant* Prince, declaring neverless that his Intention therein was that, *that of Nantes* should be inviolably kept, and accordingly kept it himself to his dying Days. But this is only intended, forsooth, to lull the Protestants asleep till a favourable Occasion to destroy them should present.

Lewis the XIV at his coming to the Crown confirms the Edict, and declares that he will maintain the reform'd in all their Privileges; he afterwards confirms in another Declaration, how highly he is satisfied with their

Services; and testifies his Design of
establishing them in the Enjoyment of
their Rights, but this is all but a meer
Amusement, and an Artifice to entrap
them, the better so to colour over the
Project of ruining them at a conven-
ient time.   What a Character now of
the most Christian Kings will this
give to the Enemies of *France*, and to
all foreign Nations?   And what confidence can they imagine will be hence-
forth put in any of their Promises
and Treaties?   For if they deal thus
with their own Subjects, and caress
'em only to ruin them, what can
Strangers expect?

Let us a little consider how they
introduce the King saying, that at his
first coming to the Crown, he was in
the Design which he has now been
just executing.   They mean without
doubt, from the time he actually took
the Reins of Government in hand,
for he was too young before, to enter
personally on any Design of this
Nature: he enter'd on it then, precisely at the time, when the Civil

Wars which had been during his Minority were ended. But what does this mean, but that he engag'd in this Design at the very time when the Protestants came from rendring him the most important Service that Subjects were ever capable of doing their Prince. They came from giving him the highest Testimonies of Loyalty imaginable, then when the greatest part of his other Subjects had taken up Arms against him, they had vigorously opposed the Progress of his Enemies; rejected the great and advantageous Offers that were made them; kept Towns, yea whole Provinces for him; took his Servants and Officers into their Bosoms, when they could not find safety elsewhere; sacrificed their Estates, their Lives, their Fortunes, and their all to him; and in a Word, done all with such a Zeal, as becomes faithful Subjects in so dangerous a Juncture. And this now is the time when the King to requite them for all this, enters on the Design of their utmost Destruction and Ex-

tirpation. This so confirms the Truth
of what we said in the Beginning,
that it puts it out of all Question:
that the Project of their Destruction
was grounded on the Services they
had rendred the King.

But is it not astonishing that we
must be taught this important Secret,
and all *Europe* besides; for although
the Protestants have done nothing in
this occasion but their *Duty*, it could
never be imagined their *Duty* should
be made their *Crime:* and their *Ruine*
should spring from whence should
come their *Safety.*   God brought
Light out of Darkness; but the Politicks of France, on the contrary Darkness out of Light.   However, they
cannot deny that in this new Edict,
the King is made to say, he entered
on the Design to destroy the Protestant Party at the very time wherein
they so signaliz'd and distinguished
themselves so successfully for the Interest of the Crown, which will furnish
thinking Men, as well within, as without the Kingdom, with matter enough

for Reflexion, and will shew them what use is made of Services and what Recompense to be expected for them.

But we shall say no more of the Expressions of the new Edict, but rather consider the *matter* of it. Was ever a worse and harder Usage than that we have suffered for the Space of above Twenty Years, which have been employed in forming the late Tempest which has at last overwhelmed us. It has been a continual Storm of Decrees, Edicts, Declarations, Orders, Condemnations of Churches, Demolitions of Temples, civil and criminal Processes, Imprisonments, Banishments, *Amendes Honourables*, pecuniary Mulcts, Privation of Offices and Employs, depriving Parents of their Children, and all those other Persecutions which we have already briefly summ'd up. We were told on one hand, that the King would continue to us the Edict of *Nantes*, and he also delivered himself on several Occasions to that Effect; and on the other hand we were made to suffer

after innumerable manners in our
Estates, in our Honours, in our Rep-
utations, in our Persons, in our Families, in our Religion, in our Consciences, and all by unjust and indirect Ways; by unheard of Inventions,
by false Witnesses, by Oppressions,
by publick Vexations, and sometimes
underhand Dealings; and all this
under the Veil of the King's Authority, and because this was his *good
pleasure.* We know very well the
Authority of Kings, and the Respect
and Submission with which we ought
to receive their Orders. And therefore
have we, during all these unsupportable Usages expressed a Patience, and
an Obedience so remarkable, that it
has been the Admiration of the
Catholicks themselves, our Country-
men. But it must be acknowledged
that those who put his Majesty on
dealing thus with us, or have used
his name and Authority for this
could not possibly do him a greater
Dishonour than they have hereby
done him, for after all, those Kings

who would be esteemed for their Justice and Equity, hardly govern their Subjects after this manner. They are not for putting all things into Confusion, or filling all Places with Horror and Despair. They seek not their Satisfaction in the Tears and Groans of the Innocent. They take no Pleasure in keeping their Subjects in a perpetual Agitation, leaving them a Life precarious from Day to Day. They love not to have their Names mentioned with Terror, nor do they meditate continual Designs of extirpating those who give them constant and unquestionable Proofs of their Loyalty; much less do they invent cruel Projects, which like Mines may destroy unseen their own natural Subjects, and this too under pretence of Kindness, by the slie and equivocal Declarations which came out then thickest just as the Blow was ready to be given.

There are 3 Things remarkable in the Conduct of this whole Affair. The first is, that as long as they were only on the Way, the true Authors of

the Persecution did not conceal themselves but always studied to conceal
the King as much as they could; 'Tis
true, the Degrees, Edicts, and Declarations and such other things went
still under the Name of his Majesty;
But *on the Request* of the Agents,
and Syndics of the Clergy: and whilst
they were busied in these Matters, the
King declar'd openly his intention of
maintaining the Edict it self, and that
'twas only the Abuses and Contraventions of it, which he design'd to
correct.

The second is, that when they came
to the last Extremities, and open force,
then they concealed themselves as
much as they could, but made the
King appear at his full Length. There
was nothing heard but these kind of
Speeches, *The King will have it so,
the King has taken the Matter in his
own hands; the King carries it further than the Clergy could have wished.*
By these Two means, they have had
the Address to be only charg'd with
the lesser and milder Part of the Per-

secution, and to lay the more violent
and odious at the King's Door.

The third thing which we are to remark is, that the better to obtain their
Ends, they have made it their Business to perswade the King, that this
Work would crown him with the highest Glory; which is a most horrid
Abuse of his Credulity, and an Abuse
so much the greater, by how much
they would skreen themselves from
being thought the Authors of this
Council. Hence, if any of them in
particular be ask'd at this Day *what
they think of it*, there are few of them
but will readily condemn it.

Now what falser Idea of Glory
could they give, than making it consist in surprizing a poor People de-
fenceless and helpless, disperst over
all his Kingdom, and living securely
under his wings and under the Protection of the Remains of the Edict
of *Nantes?* And who could ever
imagine, there were any Intentions of
depriving them, of the established
Liberty of their Consciences, of surprizing and overwhelming them in an

instant with a numerous Army, to
whose Discretion they are delivered
up; and who tell them roundly they
must either by fair means or by foul,
become Roman Catholicks, for that
such is the Kings Will and Pleasure?
What falser Notion of Glory could
they ever offer him, than the putting
him thus in the place of God, nay even
above God, in making the Faith and
Religion of his Subjects, depend on
his sole Authority, and that hence forward it must be said in his Kingdom,
I believe not because I am perswaded,
but I believe, because the King will
have me, let God say what he will,
which to speak properly is, that I believe nothing, and that I'll be a Turk,
a Jew, an Atheist, or whatever the King
pleases? What falser Idea of Glory
than to force from Men's Mouths by
Violence, and a long Series of Torments, a Confession, which the Heart
abhors, and for which they afterwards .
sigh Night and Day, crying continually to God for Mercy! What Glory is
there in inventing new Ways of Per-

secution, unknown to former Ages;
Persecutions which indeed do not
bring Death along with them, but keep
Men alive to suffer, that their Patience
and Constancy may be overcome by
Cruelties, which are above human
strength to undergo! What Glory
is there in not contenting himself to
force those who remain in his Kingdom; but to prohibit also their leaving it, and so keep them under a
double Servitude both of Soul and
Body! What Glory is there in stuff-
ing his prisons full of Innocent Persons, who are charg'd with no other
Crime than the serving God according
to the best of their Knowledge: and
for this to be exposed either to the
rage of the Dragoons, or be condemned to the Gallies, and suffer Execution on Body and Goods?

What falser Idea of Glory for the
King than to make it consist in the
Abuse of his Power, and to violate
without so much as a shadow of Reason, his own Word and Royal Faith,
which he had so solemnly given, and
so often reiterated; and this only be-

cause he can do it with impunity, and
has to deal with a Flock of Innocent
Sheep that are under his paw, and
cannot escape him; And yet 'tis this
which the Clergy of *France*, by the
Mouth of the Bishop of *Valence*, calls
a Greatness and a Glory that raises
Lewis XIV, above all other Kings,
above all his Predecessors, and above
Time it self, and consecrates him for
Eternity? 'Tis what Monsieur *Varillas* calls Labours greater and more
incredible without comparison than
those of Hercules. 'Tis what Mr.
Maimbourg calls an Heroick Action.
The Heroical Action (says he) That
the King has just now done, in forbidding by his new Edict of October
the publick Exercise of the False
Religion of the Calvinists, and order-
ing that all their Churches be forwith
demolished. Base unworthy Flatters!
Must people suffer themselves to be
blinded by the Fumes of your incense.

We should be very loth to exaggerate anything, which may violate
the Respect due to so great a Prince;

but we do not think it a failure in our
Duty; fairly to represent how far
these treacherous Counsellors and
odious Parasites, have really injured
his honour, by the sad Misfortunes
which they have plunged us into, and
how criminal they have thereby made
themselves toward his Majesty.

* They have commit-
ted no less Misdemean-
ours against their coun-
try; of which they are Members, and
for which a Man would think they
should have at least some Consideration.   Not to speak here of the great
Number of Persons of all Ages, Sexes
and Qualities, which they have cut off
from it, by their fierce Tempers; although perhaps this Loss be not so
inconsiderable as they are willing to
have it thought, it is certain that
France is a very populous Country,
but when these feaverish Fits shall be
over, and they shall in cold Blood
come to consider what they have done,
they will find with regret, that these
Diminutions are no matter of Tri-

** The Second
Reflexion.*

umph, for 'tis not possible that so
many substantial People, so many intire Families, who have made themselves considable in Arts and Sciences, civil and military, can leave a
Kingdom without one day being
miss'd! At present, whilst they re-
joyce in their Spoils, possess themselves of their Houses and Estates,
this Loss is not so much felt; 'tis
recompensed in some measure they
think, by the booty and by the ease of
maintaining the Souldiers by this
Plunder, but this will not always hold.
Neither shall we here insist on that
almost general Interruption of Traf-
fick, which these most *Unchristian
Persecutors* have caused in the principal Towns of the Kingdom, although
this be no little Misfortune. The Protestants carried on a good part of the
Trade, as well within the Kingdom as
without; and were therein so mixt
with the Roman Catholicks, that
their Affairs were in a manner in-
separably linked together, they dealt
as it were in common when these
Oppressions came upon them. And

what Confusions have they not produced? How many industrious Measures have they broken? How many
honest Designs have they not disap-
pointed? How many Manufactures
have been ruin'd? How many bank-
rupts have they made? And how
many Families reduced to Beggary?
But this is what the Oppressors little
trouble themselves about, they have
their Bread gain'd to their Mouths,
they live in Wantonness and Ease:
and whilst others starve for Hunger,
their Revenues are ascertain'd to
them. But this hinders not, but that
the Body of the Estate must still suffer, both in its *Honour and Interest.*
And we may truly say, that Four
Civil Wars could not have produced
so much mischief, as time will shew to
spring from this one Persecution alone.

But we will leave the Consequence
of this Affair to Time, and only say,
that the Edict of *Nantes*, being a fundamental Law of the Kingdom, and
an Agreement between Two Parties
by a reciprocal Acceptation, under the

peaceable Reign of *Henry the Great* by the publick Faith, and by mutual Oath, this must certainly be highly Disadvantagious to the Interest of the State, and a very bad Precedent, that after having made a Thousand Infractions of it, it should at length be revok'd, cancell'd and annull'd at the Instigation of a Cabal, who abuse their Credit, and hereby make themselves fit for enterprising and executing any thing.   After this Violation, what can henceforward be thought firm and inviolable in *France*, I speak not only of particular Men's Affairs, or of private Families, but of general Establishments, of Royal Companies, of Courts of Justice, of fundamental Laws and Constitutions, and in one word of whatever may relate to the Order, either of judicial Proceedings, or of the Affairs of State, or may serve for a Basis and Foundation of Society; even the Inalienable Rights of the Crown, and the Form of Government it self, not excepted: which are all hereby manifestly shaken.

There are in the Kingdom of *France* a great many thinking Men to whom it will not be hard to discern this. There are, I say, a great Number of worthy Persons in it, who understand how to think as they ought of Matters, and whose Eyes are opened. I mean not your Poets, or such sort of fulsome Flatterers, who for the Sake of a few Madrigals, or a Panegyrick perhaps upon the King, run away with considerable Preferments, and Benefices : nor your Authors who are prepared to write on any side, be it right or wrong, without any Consideration for the true Merit of the Cause; and who are elevated with their knowledge, as if they indeed knew every thing, when they know not how little and contemptible they really are. For I am speaking of those wise, solid, and penetrating Spirits, who look a great way into the Consequences of Things, and are able to make a right Judgment upon them.

Shall we think that these Men see

not what is too visible, namely, that
the State is pierced, through and
through, by the same Thrust given the
Protestants, and that such an open
Revocation of the Edict, with so
high an hand, leaves nothing firm
and sacred.

It is to no purpose to alledge
Distinctions in the matter, or say,
that the pretended reformed Religion
was odious to the State, and that
therefore this Attack was with the
more Freedom made, for not to
mention that the Example is so much
the more dangerous, as it was the
more cunningly pitched on, in an
Affair, wherein the People are likely
to take little or no Concern: without
adding that their having rendred the
Reformed Religion odious to the
People, was for certain a premeditated Preparation to what they intended to execute afterwards, and
also that far from having a general
Aversion against our Religion, the
Catholicks both the Common People
and the Nobility had no manner of

Animosity against us, (except only a Faction of' the Bigots, and those that are call'd the *Propagators of the Faith*) but on the contrary pitied us, and condoled our Misfortunes.

Not to touch further on this, who knows not what an easy matter it is to run down any Cause, or render it odious, or at least indifferent, in the minds of the people, there are never wanting Reasons and Pretences, in matters of this Nature, one Party is set up against another; and that is call'd the *State*, right or wrong, which is the prevailing one : like as in Religion, not the best and holiest, *but the powerfullest and boldest Part is term'd the Church.* We must not then judge of these things from the *Matter*, but from the Form. Now if there ever was since the World stood, any thing most solid or inviolable, it was surely this Edict of *Nantes ;* to revoke and cancel it, is then to set ones self up above all Obligations to God as well as to Men, 'tis to declare openly,

that there are no longer any Ties or
Promises obligatory in the World,
but that all things are at pleasure
revokable, this is no more than the
wise will easily comprehend; and I
doubt not but they have comprehended it already.

But it will be proper here to present another Objection, which is, that
as the Edict, (take it in what sense
we will) is become only a Law by the
Authority of *Henry the Great*, so it
may likewise be revok'd and annull'd
by that of *Lewis* XIV. his Grandson,
and Successor. For there is no more
Difficulty in one, than in the other:
for 'tis easy for Kings to determine
by the same means as they began,
since if *Henry the Great* had Power
to change the Form of governing
the State, by introducing into it a
new Law; why has not Lewis the
XIV. the same power then to alter
this Form, and by Consequence annul whatsoever his Grandfather has
done? But this Objection is but a
meer Fallacy, and will be soon an-

swered by considering that it's built upon a false Principle, and thence deduces a falser Conclusion. For as to the Principle upon which this is founded, we say it was not the single Authority of *Henry the Great* which established the Edict. The Edict was a Decree of his Justice after all Parties were heard, and a concordate that pass'd between the Catholicks and the Reformed, authoriz'd by the publick Faith of the whole Estate, confirmed with the Sanction of an Oath, and ratified by the Execution of it; now this is it that renders the Edict immutable, and sets it above the Reach of any of the Successors of *Henry* the IV. They can be only in this Case, the Depositaries and the Executors, not the Masters of it, and can have no Right to make it depend on their absolute Will and Pleasure. *Henry the Great* never employed the Force of Arms to make the Catholicks consent to it; and though since his Death under the Minority of Louis XIII. There

have been several Assemblies of the
State of the Realm, the Edict has still
remained in its full Force and Vigor,
it was therefore, as we have already
said, a fundamental Law of the Kingdom, which the King by his own proper
Authority could have no Ground of
Right to touch. But then even supposing this were a Work grounded on
the bare Authority of *Henry*, which
in Fact is false; it does not therefore
follow that his present Majesty can
lawfully revoke it. And the Reason
hereof is evident, because there are
many things which depend on the
good Pleasure of Kings to *do*, but
which when done, do not depend on
the same good Pleasure to undo; and
of this Nature is the said Edict.

It is a Royal Promise, which *Henry
the Great* made to the Reformed of
his Kingdom, as well for himself as
his Successors for ever, and consequently this is a perpetual Obligation or hereditary Debt, charged on
himself and his Posterity. Moreover,
it is not true that *Henry the Great*

did change any thing in the Government of the State, at least as to Essentials, when he gave Liberty of Conscience to his Subjects; for this Liberty is a Matter of more Ancient and more inviolable Right than all Edicts, seeing that it is a Right of Nature.

He permitted a publick Exercise of the Reformed Religion; but this Exercise was establish'd in the Kingdom before his Edict, and if he has enlarged the privilege of the Reformed, as (without doubt he has,) he did not do it without the Consent and Approbation of the State, and so herein violated nothing of his lawful Engagements.

But now 'tis not the same with *Lewis* XIV. who of his own pure Authority, makes a real and fundamental Change against the Concurrence of *one* Part of his People, and without the consulting of the *other;* hereby violating his own most sacred Engagements, those of his Kingdom, and even the Laws of Nature too,

which were things absolutely out of
his Power to do.

In short, if we consider the means
that have been used to arrive at the
Revocation in Question, it will be impossible for a Man not to acknowledge
how the State is sensibly hurt thereby.
For as if it were not enough to suppress the Religious Assemblies, and
to null the Privileges and civil Rights
of the Protestants, by unjust Decrees,
without so much as any Formality or
Hearing; There are also sent among
the *Souldiers to dispute the Points of
Religion with them;* and oblige them
to turn.   They are sackt like People
taken by Assault, they are forc'd in
their Consciences, and Hell itself, with
all that is merciless and cruel is let
loose upon them for this End.   And
this is to speak modestly, *The effect*
of a Military and Arbitrary *Government*, which is *regulated neither by
Justice, Reason nor Humanity.*   Can
it be thought, that *France* will find its
Account in this matter !   Or that wise
Men will think this an equitable Way

of governing? However, this is a first Essay that is none of the least, they that made it, shew how skilful they are, and who knows if they will be content to rest here? There needs only another design, another Passion to satisfie, another Revenge to execute; and then woe be to those who shall oppose it, for the Dragoons will not have forgot their Trade.

The Third Reflexion. * To these two Reflexions, which Respect the *French* King and the States of his Realm, we may add a *Third* which will regard the Interests of all the Kings, Princes, and other Potentates of *Europe*, as well of the one as of the other Religion. We shall not be much mistaken if we say, that they have a common and general Concern herein; in as much as these most skilful Artists in Mischief do as much as ever they can to trouble the good Understanding that is between them and their Subjects. We are however perswaded, that their wise and just Government will, in this Respect put them out of all fear: But

this hinders not Examples of this
Nature from being always of bad
Consequence, as naturally tending to
beget in the Minds of the Vulgar,
(who commonly judge of things without examining into particulars) Suspi-
cions and Distrusts of their Sover-
eigns, as if they dreamed of nothing
but devouring their Subjects, and de-
livering them up to the Discretion (or
rather Fury) of their Souldiers.   For
the greater Moderation and Justice
Princes may have, the less are they
obliged to such as would inspire their
People with matter for so dangerous
Sentiments; which are apt to produce
the worse Effects.

Besides is it not certain, that the
Princes and States of *Europe*, cannot
without a great deal of Displeasure
see *France*, which makes so considerable a figure in the World, and has so
powerful an Influence, should now put
her self in such a Condition as that no
just Measures can be taken with her?
For after so scandalous and publick a
Violation of the Word of Three suc-

cessive Kings, and of the publick Faith, what credit can be ever given for the future, to her Promises, or Treaties? Nor will it be sufficient here to say, that the publick Treaties will have force, so long at least as the Interest of *France* will require, for that will hereafter depend on the private Interest, or perhaps capriciousness, of a sort of heady strong People, that are for allowing nothing either to the Laws of Prudence or of Equity, but will manage all by main Force.

And if they have had the Power to do within the Kingdom what they have lately put in Execution, what may we not expect that they will do as to Affairs abroad? If they have not spar'd their own Countrymen, with whom they had daily Commerce, and who were greatly serviceable to them, can it be supposed they will spare such as are altogether Strangers? Will they have more Respect think you to Truces or Agreements but of yesterday, than to an Edict of an

Hundred Years continuance, and that too the most august and solemn that ever was; which yet they made no other use of than to amuse an innocent People, and to involve them the more securely in utter Desolation? It looks truly as if they had resolved to bring Matters to this pass on purpose, that their being no more Faith or Dependency to be had on the promises of *France*, all her Neighbours should thereby continually be upon their Guard against her; and the more when she promises than when she threatens; and in Peace than in War, so that there is no more Hopes of being at quiet with Respect to her, but what either the Security of Hostages, or the Diminution of her Forces must give. This being so in Respect of all Princes and States in general, as well Catholick as Protestant, what may then the Protestant Princes and States in particular think, but that it is really the Design of *France* to ruin them all, and to make no stop till she has utterly devoured them?

Everybody knows, that the Protestant Princes and Powers understand
their Interests well enough, to be able
to discern them through the Clouds,
and Mists wherewith these would
cover them, and 'tis not doubted but
they do indeed see, that this is a Beginning, or an Essay, which *France*
expects shortly to give the last and
finishing Stroak to.

That Court has suffered itself to be
possessed with a most gross Bigotry,
and with a false Zeal of Catholicism;
it is become the *Genius* that pleases;
each one is become a converter even
to Fire and Sword: and there are not
a few of the Courtiers perswaded that
this shall be alone able to weigh down
the Scale in their Favour, vain glory
is no small Ingredient in this Design;
Policy adds also its Prospects and
Misteries too, and as these prospects
have no Bounds, so these Misteries
want not their invisible Springs and
surprising Ways, which they will joyn
when they please, to the Power of
Arms.   They think the Season is

ripe, and 'tis but daring to go on.   The
Easiness they found in making Con-
quests and Conversions swells their
Courage, and they talk already of
nothing but a further Progress in so
fair a Way.   'Tis however to be
hoped that Protestant Princes, and
States, will from hence draw their just
Conclusions.

As to the Catholick Princes and
States they have too sagacious Judgments not to see how much they share
also in this Affair.   It will *be* made
use of to break the good understanding which is betwixt them and the
Protestant Powers by amusing *those*
with the fair Pretext of the Catholick
Religion, and cunningly inspiring
these with Suspitions and Jealousies
of a general Design against them, to
swallow 'em.   If the Catholick Princes and States remove not these Suspitions, and if they suffer *France* still
to aggrandize her self, by her pretended Zeal for the Catholick Faith,
which at the Bottom is but a false
Mask, one may without the Spirit of

Prophesy aforehand assure them that they are undone.

It will signify but little to say, *we are as good Catholicks as yourselves*, this will be no Security from his Army; whosoever will not submit to his Yoke shall be an Heretick, nay worse than an Heretick; for now the greatest Heresy *is not to submit:* *Spain, Germany*, and *Italy* it self, already know this in some measure.

But will it not be thought a Paradox, if to all that we have said we yet farther add, that even the *Pope* himself,* and the *whole* Body of the *Roman Church*, must find themselves sensibly interress'd and injur'd in this Persecution. And yet we will say nothing herein, but what is evident Truth, and which the wisest of the Roman Catholicks, must needs agree to. For is not this the worst Character that can be given of the Roman Clergy, to Represent them as an Order of Men, who not only can't endure any thing that is not subject to

* *The Fourth Reflexion.*

them in a Religious, but also in a
Civil Society, and as Men that are not
content to anathematize all that dis-
please them, but who design nothing
so much as to exterminate 'em, not
only to exterminate them but also
forcibly to violate their Consciences,
and cram their own Opinions down
their Throats, and propagate their
Way of Worship by the irresistible
and never-failing Argument of Fire
and Fagot; lastly as an Order of Men
who observe neither Faith nor Justice; who promise only that they may
deceive, who for awhile curb their
Fury only, that afterwards they may
insult the more; that in Peace as well
as in War, contrive only to overturn
and destroy; who make Allyances
only to surprize, and then finding
themselves more powerful, deny those
they have so surprised even the Liberty of escaping. These are the
exact Features and Colours by which
the *Roman Clergy* may be easily
known, should we Judge of them by
the Persecution in *France;* the like
whereof was never seen to this Day.

The *Egyptians* and *Assyrians* once persecuted the *Israelites*, but forced them not to embrace the Worship of their Idols; they contented themselves with making them slaves, without doing Violence to their Consciences. The *Heathens* and the Jews persecuted the primitive Christians, forced their consciences indeed, but they had never granted them an Edict, nor by persecuting them violated the publick Faith, nor hindred them to make their Escape by Flight. The *Arrians* cruelly persecuted the *Orthodox*, but besides that they went not so far, as to make the common sort of People sign formal Abjurations; there was no Edict, or Concordat between the Two Communions. *Innocent* the III. by his Croisades persecuted the *Waldenses* and *Albigenses*, but neither had these People any Edict. *Emmanuel* King of *Portugal* furiously persecuted the *Jews*, but he gave them leave to depart out of his Kingdom, and they too had no Edict. It was the same with those Remains of the Moors, who had canton'd themselves in some parts of the Kingdom of *Grenada;* they were defeated in a War, and commanded to retire into the Country from whence their Ancestors came.

In the last Century the Duke *D'Alba* exercised dreadful Cruelties, upon the Protestants of the seventeen Provinces, but he did not hinder them from flying, nor violated any Edict; and when the worst came to the worst, Death was their release. The *Inquisition* is to this Day in *Spain* and *Italy;* but they are Countries in which no Religion, besides the Roman, was ever tolerated by Edicts, and if the Inquisitors may be accused of Violence and Cruelty, they cannot however be convicted of Perfidiousness.

But in this last Persecution of *France,* there are *Five* things that strike the Mind with Horror.   1st. they make the Consciences and Religion of Men to depend soveraignly upon the Will of a mortal King, 2dly

they violate a Faith solemnly sworn
to. 3dly they force Men to be Hypo-
crites and oblige them to be wicked,
by seeming to embrace a Religion
they abhor, 4thly they prohibit and
prevent All Flight and Retiring out of
the Kingdom, 5thly they do not inflict
Death but preserve Life for no other
purpose than to oppress it with longer
and more dreadful *Torments*.   If after
this the Court of *Rome* with its
Clergy, dispers'd all over *Europe*,
will not disclaim so odious and criminal a conduct, nay if they condemn it
not it will be an indelible Stain to
the Honour of their Religion.   For
not only Protestants, who are of a different Communion, but also an infinite
Number of their own Members, will
be mightily scandalized thereat, nay
even *Turks*, *Jews*, and *Pagans* will
rise up in Judgment against them.
They cannot be ignorant what Cen-
sures have been made on what pass'd
in the Council of *Constance* concerning *John Huss* and *Jerom* of *Prague*,
whom they put to Death, notwithstanding the safe Conduct of the Em-

peror *Sigismund*.   But there is some-
thing greater here: There only Two
Men were concern'd, *here* more than
Fifteen Hundred Thousand, those
they put to Death, and if they had
done the same to *these*, they would
have embraced their Death with Joy
and Comfort.   The Council thought
its Authority in this greater than the
Emperors, but here can be produced
none greater than that which establish'd our Edict.

 * We are not insen-
sible of the different
Methods the Persecu-
tors take to shelter
themselves from public Censure, some
take a speedy course, that is down-
right to deny the Fact, and to perswade the World, That Force and
Violence had no share in the conversions; but that they were soft, calm,
and voluntary; and that if there were
some Dragoons at any time concern'd
therein, 'twas only because the Reformed themselves desired 'em, that
so they might have an handsom Pretence of changing their Religion.

*Refutation of
the false Shifts
and Pretences
of the Persecutors.*

Was their ever so much Impudence seen! What will they not deny, who can thus flatly deny what was done in the Face of the Sun, and what a whole Kingdom from one End of it, to the other have seen, and still see to this Day? For now in the Beginning of the Year 1686, While I am composing this sad Narrative, they continue to exercise the very same Rage, that concluded the preceding Year; the same Dragoons both in Cities and Countries execute the same Fury against some miserable Remains of Protestants, who will not fall down and worship the Golden Image.

They are used like Rebels in their Persons, in their Estates, in their Wives and in their Children; and if there be any difference, 'tis in this that their Sufferings are still increas'd, yet if we will believe the Clergy haranguing the King by the Mouth of the Bishop of *Valence* their Speaker, it is a Miracle of his Majesty's Reign that such infinite Numbers should be by him converted without using any constraint at all, and that from all

Parts, there should be such a Con-
course of People joyfully flocking to
re-unite themselves to the Catholick
Church, *All this*, saith he, *is done
without Violence*, without arms, and
not so much by the force of your
Edicts, as by the Explariness of
your Piety.   And if we will believe
moreover the greatest Part of the Abjurations which these poor opprest
People, are forc'd to make with a
Dagger at their Breast; they speak
indeed the same Sense, that is, that
they have done this of their own
proper Motion, without being constrained in any wise thereto.

If we will believe *Monsieur Maimbourg* in his Epistle Dedicatory to
the King, which he has prefixed, before his History of Pope *Gregory*
lately Publish'd, there has been neither
Arms nor Violence used for those
Conversions, You are to believe, says
he, that after having already van-
quished all the Enemies of France
by the invincible Power of your Arms,
you shall alone eternally have the
Glory and Happiness of having rooted

out of the most Christian Kingdom, that Enemy of God, Heresy (as he calls it), without using against it, to compel the Protestants to return into the Bosom of the Church, other Arms, or Forces, than those of your most charitable Zeal for their Conversion, and the manifest Justice of your Decrees and Edicts, which have had all the Success as could be wish'd for or expected. And in his *third* Book after having said that *Ethelred* King of England did not compel by any kind of Violence his Subjects to embrace the Christian Religion, having learned of his Divines that the Service rendred to Jesus Christ ought to be voluntary, but only kept his Favours for such as should turn Christians, without doing Injustice to others; after this he adds these Words; This is the Method Lewis the Great follows exactly at this time in order to convert the pretended Reformed, who have no Cause of Complaint. For no Violence is offer'd to anyone, and if the King be graciously pleased to bestow on the new Converts, such Favours and Kindness

as are not bestow'd upon others, and
which he is not obliged to confer upon
those who are obstinate in their Heresy; yet no injustice is hereby done,
since nothing of any Privilege is taken
from them, but what they have usurped
contrary to the intent of the Edicts;
and that he has a Right to Punish
them, when they act contrary to his
Ordinances. It is very likely that this
Method so soft, so prudent, so effica-
cious will at last have the same effect
in France under Lewis the Great, to
reconcile the Calvinists to the Church
as it had under King Ethelred in England for the Conversion of his Subjects;
who powerfully drawn by such means
came dayly crowding to demand the
holy Baptism, as we see our Protestants,
begin now to come in Flocks to Mass.

And 'tis upon the same Principles
that Monsieur Varillas in his Ded-
ication to the King of the Book
just publish'd by him under the
Title of the History of the Revolu-
tions which have happen'd in Europe
in Matters of Religion, does not scruple to speak in this manner; Your

Majesty in order to ruin Calvinism
has only obliged the French that
profess'd it, to the exact Observance of
the Edict of Nantes; by punishing the
Contraventions with the Penalties con-
tain'd therein; that alone was sufficient
to reduce the Hereticks to so small a
Number, that the Edict being now useless there was reason to revoke it.

Thus is the Credulity of the Publick wretchedly impos'd on, the Seeds
of Imposture are sown at Random,
which are left to grow up, and matur-
ate with time. Posterity who shall
see these pieces of pretended Histories, will be apt to believe them True.
And making their Judgment from
this surprizing account of the matter,
they will certainly say. Behold here
what has been said to the King himself, who must not have open False-
hoods presented to him; here also
are the proper Acts and Deeds of
those very Persons who were converted. Why shall not then Posterity believe it; seeing that even at present
there are some Shameless enough, (or

to speak better, well enough Paid)
to Publish it in foreign Countries;
and that there are found likewise some
credulous enough to believe it.

And why should they not believe it,
seeing it is asserted by a Bishop; and
that in the Name too of the Body of
the Clergy, and by Two grave Authors
besides? Must there be so much
said to establish a *probable* Opinion?
Posterity will not be bound to know
who this Bishop of Valence was; nor
what sort of a Life he always led; nor
will they be under a necessity of
knowing how many Fables Monsieur
Maimbourg has been more than once
convicted of; which he had embelish'd
his Histories with, nor that he was a
Person determinately Resolv'd, though
detected, never to acknowledge himself in an Error, neither will they be
oblig'd to know, that Monsieur *Varillas* not finding his Account in telling
the Truth, has in his old Days thought
fit at last, to consecrate his Pen to this
Service, induc'd to it by the Favors
of the Archbishop of Paris, as may

be gather'd from the Preface of this his late Treatise.

But to come to the Point, what likelihood is there that so great and considerable a Number of Persons, should without anything constraining them to it, chuse to Fly out of *France*, and leave behind them their Houses, their Lands of Inheritance, their Effects, and several of them too their Wives and Children, only for to rove about the World, and lead a miserable Life out of meer Humour: Is there any likelihood that Persons of Quality of both Sexes, who enjoyed some Twelve, Fifteen, Twenty, or Thirty Thousand Livres *per Annum*, should abandon their Estates, and that not only for themselves but for their Successors too: Expose themselves to numberless Perils, and to the Inconveniences of long Journies; and reduce themselves in a manner to Beggary; which is a Condition the most unsupportable in the World to Persons of Quality, and all this without any Reason, Purely out of a Frolick and, for the sake of a Jest,

without any Occasion? What likelihood that about an Hundred and
Fifty Thousand Persons who have
already escap'd; some of them into
Switzerland, others into *Germany*,
some into *England*, others into *Holland*, some into *Swedeland*, and others
into *Denmark*, and some even into
America, without having ever seen
or known one another, should yet all
agree to tell the same Lie, and to say
with one Voice, that the Protestants
are cruelly persecuted in France, and
that by unheard of Severities they are
forc'd to change their Religion; although there is no such Matter, is it
likely in the last Place, that the Em-
·bassadors and Envoys of foreign Princes and Powers, should all of them
Lie in concert to their Masters; telling them such things which had no
Foundation of Truth?

But again, if in *France* the Protestants thus voluntarily, and without constraint, change their Religion, and
that the Dragoons are call'd in only
as Friends, whence comes it that there
is so strict and universal a Guard, on

the Frontiers, to hinder their with-
drawing? How is it that the Prisons
are cram'd with those who endeavouring to make their Escape, were stopt
by the Way? Whence is it that those
who have chang'd their Religion, are
watched with so great care to hinder
their Flight, even to the obliging them
to Deposit good Sums of Money, to
secure them from the Suspition of it?
What an epidemical Distemper is
there raging among his Majesty's
Subjects, that should make them
Fly thus without Reason or without
Grounds? and is not this a pleasant
shift to say, that the Protestants have
themselves call'd in the Dragoons to
have a better pretence to change their
Religion?

'Tis about Ten Years or more, since
there was a Bank set up for Souls:
Mr. *Pelisson* has been for a long time
at *Paris*, the great Dealer in this infamous Trade of purchasing Converts.
These Conversions have of late been
the only way of getting Applause,
and into Preferments at Court, and in

a Word, a sure and effectual means of
raising ones Fortune; And yet they
would fain make People think us such
Fools, as that in stead of being converted by these easie and advantageous
Methods, we should rather choose the
help of Dragoons, that is to have the
Pleasure of being pillag'd at the best;
at least let any one tell us, why, since
these Conversions are all pretended
to be *Voluntary*, upon the Peoples not
being to go to Mass, they should have
sent the Dragoons to visit them a
Second Time, and use them with the
same severity as before.

This is indeed so gross and palpa-
ble a lie that others who are more In-
genuous have undertaken to defend
these Violences, as if they were naturally from the genuine Spirit of the
Catholick Church; and for this Purpose, they have continually in their
Mouth that Passage of the Gospel,
Compelle Intrare, compel them to come
in; the Letter of St. *Augustin* to *Vin-
centius* and the Persecution by the *Orthodox* of *Africk* against the *Donatists-*

Were this a Place to dispute against those furious Theologists, 'twould not be hard to shew the Vanity of those Allegations, the Apostles knew at least as well as they, the Sence and Intent of their Master, neither wanted they Zeal for the Promotion of his Gospel. Did they therefore ever make use of Arms to augment the Number of the Faithful, or did their Master for that end give them any Temporal or Military power? Who knows not but in the Stile of Scripture the Words *Compellere* and *Cogere* signifie a soft Violence of Exhortation and Persuasion, as in the XIX of *Genesis*, where it is said that *Lot compelled* the Angels to come into his House, *Compulit illos oppido* pressed upon, V. 3. and 1. Sam. XXVIII. 23. that *Saul's* Servants *Compelled* him to eat, *Coegerunt eum.* And Luke XXIV. 29, that the Two Disciples going to *Emmaus; compelled* Jesus or constrained him (Cogerunt illum) to remain with them ; and Acts XVI. 15. that Lydia *compelled* (constrained)

St. Paul and his Company (*Coegit nos*)
to come into her House.   As for St.
Augustin's Letter, it must be confess'd that nothing can better shew
us the Character of this sort of Persons than this Allegation of theirs.
They cannot be Ignorant how that
the general Sentiment of the Fathers
is, that Conscience is never to be
forced, nor Religion to be established
by Violence.   They know that this is
the general Voice of the Primitive
Church, insomuch that St. Martin cut
off from his Communion the Bishops
that persecuted the Priscilianists.
And yet these Men would fain force
upon us for a Rule of Christian Practice a Letter of one who had been
exasperated, and who had suffer'd
himself to be misled by some other
turbulent Bishops; whose Doctrine
and Reputation by this one single
Act, have been stain'd with an irreparable Blemish.   They are not a whit
more successful in what they allege,
concerning the Persecution of the
Donatists by the Orthodox.   For to
omit that the Orthodox never forced

the Donatists, either to embrace
Doctrines, or Worship that they had
an abhorence for, or to abjure those
they profess'd, they only constrained
them to submit outwardly to a personal Judgment, given by Lawful
Judges on a Matter of Fact; which
was whether *Cecilian* was a Prevari-
cator, or not.   To omit all this, I say,
it is certain that that Persecution
was visibly follow'd with Exemplary
Chastisements from the Divine Justice upon the Persecutors; who were
soon after by the *Arrians* treated with
much more Cruelty than the Donatists had been by them, thus God permitted, that as they had abus'd the
Weakness of *Honorius*, to make him
put in Execution what *Constantine* the
Great would never Consent to, so the
Arrian Bishops should in like manner
abuse the Power of the Kings of the
Vendals to oppress the flourishing
Churches of *Africa*.   But what need
of all this dispute, since all they advance is altogether besides the Question?   Let them but shew us one only

Passage, or Example, from whence it
can be inferr'd that public Faith given
to a Society by Solemn Edicts and
Treaties (such as were in the Edict of
Nantes) might be violated, had there
ever been an Agreement betwixt the
Jews and the *Heathens*, with the
Apostles, and this solemnly consented
to and ratified, when our blessed
Saviour said *Compelle Intrare* Luke
XIV. v. 23. compel them to come in;
has St. Augustin ever said, that we
ought to deal perfidiously with those
whom we esteem Hereticks, when we
have promis'd to Live with them like
Brethren, and fellow Citizens? Had
the Donatists any Edicts to shelter
them from the insults of the Orthodox? Should we yield to this detestable Divinity, what would become of
all of us? For in short the Papists
are as much Hereticks to the Protestants as the Protestants are to the Papists; yet in most parts of *Europe*,
they live together in Peace, on the
Faith of Alliances, Treaties and Promises, and trading together, are at full

Liberty to follow the Dictates of their own Consciences. But these publick Priests as much as in them lies would quickly bring all things into confusion, and a *State of War*. They set the Catholicks against the Protestants, teaching them, that their Religion obliges them to betray and surprise the Protestants, when ever they can do it safely and to treat them with Fire and Faggot, if they will not change their religion. They set the Protestants against the Catholics; for what Peace and Society can there be with People, who not only make no Conscience to break their Faith, but on the contrary think themselves obliged in Conscience to break it, as often as they find Occasion, such are the natural Consequences of the pernicious Doctrine of these Converters, with their *compelle intrare* and the letter of St. *Augustin*.

The worst on it is, these are not only the Discourses or Writings of some giddy brained Authors, whose Sphere of Activity commonly extends

no further than their Study: They
are real Deeds and notorious Facts,
'tis a great *King* whom they have
abused; powerful *Ministers* into
whose Minds they have instill'd those
Maxims, and who put 'em in practice,
Armies of *Dragoons*, who have de-
populated a whole Kingdom, and
plunder'd above Five Hundred Thousand Families.   Do we live in an Age
wherein Religion is made to consist
in having no Fear of God, or must
we imagine that the Fear of God, consists in that furious Zeal, which in-
spires such sorts of Violences? Can
any think these Excesses are pleasing
to Christ, whom we both profess to
own as the Author of our Faith, and
that he can ever be willing to have
his Religion propagated, by such
treacherous and wicked Devices? He
has said indeed, that he will not suffer
the Gates of Hell to prevail against
his Church; but he has no where said,
he will open Hell Gates for the prop-
agating of it.   Now if ever anything
in the World may be said to carry

the Air of the Gates of Hell, certainly it must be this Persecution
in *France.*

Whatever Antipathy there may be
between the See of Rome, and us, we
cannot believe the present Pope *Innocent* XII. to have had any hand
therein, or that the Storm has faln on
us from that Quarter. We know him
to be a mild Prince, and his Temper
disposed to more moderate Councils,
than those of his Predecessors. Moreover, we know the Clergy of *France* do
not always consult him in what they
set about, and what has been done by
them against *Rome*, and the little deference pay'd to its Authority has been
frequently made an Argument to induce us, to submit ourselves to the
King's Will in these other matters.
So that we hope the Pope himself
considering us still as Men, and as
Christians, will pity us, and blame
the Methods that have been used
against us, had he no other Reason
than the mere interest of his own
Religion.

However, 'tis certain the Protestants of *France* are the fittest objects of Publick Compassion, the World ever knew. Some of them Sigh and Lament under an hard and barbarous Slavery, which they would willingly exchange for Irons in *Algiers* or *Turkey*, for there they would not be forced to turn *Mahometants*, and might still entertain some hopes of Liberty by the way of Ransom. Other of them are wand'ring about in Foreign Countries, stript of their Estates, separated (in all probability for ever) from their Parents, Relations and Friends whom they have left in the most doleful condition imaginable, Husbands have left their Wives, and Wives, their Husbands, Fathers their Children, and Children their Fathers. We have seen as in a moment our Fortunes, our Establishments, our Inheritances, our Houses, our Commerce, our hopes drop away; And of all the good things of this earthly State, we have scarce any thing left us, but our miserable Lives, and they too supported by the Charity of our Christian Brethren.

Yet amongst all these Afflictions we have this Comfort still, that we truly suffer for a good Conscience, and the Cause of God, and can defy even the malice of our Persecutors, to charge us with any the least Misdemeanour that could have merited this barbarous usage; We have served our King and Country with the utmost Zeal and Fidelity; We have constantly submitted ourselves to the Laws, and to the Magistrates; We have been always ready to bear our Part of the Publick Burthens; And as for our Country Men, they have no reason to complain of us. We have for Twenty Years together suffered with an Exemplary Patience the most furious and Dreadful Storms, and when in the *Vivares* and *Cevennes*, some thought themselves bound in Conscience to Preach on the Ruines of their Churches, unjustly and illegally demolisht; their small number, which were but a handful only served to stir up more the Obedience and Resignation of the whole Body.

And in these last Storms we have been like Sheep, Innocent and without defence. We comfort our selves then in the Justice of our Cause, and in our peaceable Deportment under it.

But we comfort our selves likewise in the *Christian* Compassion shewed us by Foreign Princes, and States, who have opened their Arms and received us into their Dominions, succour'd, relieved, and comfort'd us; And the People who live under their Government, have seconded these their kind Offices. And we have found in all of them, not only new *Masters* and new *Friends*, but the real Tenderness of Fathers and Brethren. And as these Bowels of Commiseration have been as Balm to our Wounds; So we hope never to lose the Remembrance thereof, and trust, that neither we nor our Children after us, shall ever do any thing by God's Grace, to render us unworthy of this their Protection.

The only affliction for which we

cannot be comforted is, to see our Religion oppressed in the Kingdom of *France*; So many Churches, wherein God was daily served according to the simplicity of the Gospel, demolished, so many Flocks dispers'd, so many poor Consciences Sighing and Groaning under their Bondage; so many Children depriv'd of the Education they were to receive from their Parents. But we hope that at length, the same God who heard heretofore the Sighs of his People under the Bondage of *Egypt*, will also hear at this time the Cries of his Faithful Servants. We call not for Fire from Heaven, we only pray, that God would touch the Hearts of our Persecutors, that they may repent, and be saved together with us; We entreat such a Deliverance, as he in his Wisdom shall think fitting. And as our Prayers are in the Order of his Providence; We have grounds to hope that he will hear them and that he will Establish us again in our first Estate.

But in the mean while, and till it shall please God in his mercy to bring that happy Event to pass, least we should be wanting to the Justice of our Cause, we desire that this Account which contains our *Just Complaints*, may serve for a Protestation before Heaven and Earth against all the violences we have suffer'd in the Kingdom of *France.* Against all the Arrests, Declarations, Edicts, Regulations, and all other Ordinances of what nature soever, which our Enemys have caused to be Published to the prejudice of the Edict of *Nantes ;* Against all sort of Acts, Signatures, or Verbal Declarations expressing an Abjuration of our, and the Profession of the *Romish* Religion, which Fear, Torture, and a Superior Power have extorted from us or from our Brethren; Against the Plunder that has been already or shall hereafter be committed of our Goods, Houses, Effects, Debts, Trusts, Rents, Lands, Inheritances and Revenues, Common or Private, either by way of Confisca-

tion, or by any other way whatsoever
as Unjust, Treacherous, and Violent,
committed only by a Superior Power,
in full Peace, contrary both to Reason
and the Laws of Nature, and the
Rights of all Society, and injurious
to all Mankind; But especially we
Protest against the Edict of the 18th
of *October* 1685, containing the Revocation of the Edict of Nantes, as a
manifest Abuse of the King's Justice,
Authority and Royal Power, since the
Edict of Nantes was in it self inviolable and irrevocable, above the reach
of any Human Power, design'd for a
standing Agreement and Concordat
between the *Roman Catholicks*, and us,
and a fundamental Law of the Realm,
which no Authority on Earth has Power to Infringe, or Annul. We protest
likewise against all the Consequences
that may follow such a Revocation,
against the Extinction of the Exercise of our Religion throughout the
whole Kingdom of *France*, against all
the Ignominies and Cruelties committed upon dead Bodies, by depriv-

ing them of Christian Burial, and ex-
posing them in the Field to be Devoured by Ravenous Beasts, or drag-
ging them ignominiously through the
Streets upon Hurdles; against the
taking away Children by force, and
the Orders given to Fathers and
Mothers to Cause them to be Baptized and Educated by *Romish* Priests.
But above all. we *Protest* against that
impious and abominable Position,
which is now adays made the General
Rule in *France*, by which Religion is
made to depend on the Pleasure and
Despotick Power of a Mortal Prince,
and Perseverance in the Faith branded
with the Names of Rebellion and
Treason, which is to make of a Man
a God, and tends to the introducing and authorizing of Atheism
and Idolatry. We *Protest* moreover
against all manner of violent and
inhumane detaining of our Brethren
in *France*, whether in Prisons, Gallies, Monasteries, or any other Con-
finements, to hinder them from
leaving the Kingdom, and going to

seek in Foreign Countries that Liberty of Conscience which they cannot enjoy in their own; which is the utmost pitch of Brutish Cruelty and Hellish Iniquity.

Lastly we *Protest* against whatsoever we may, of Right Protest against, and declare that such is our meaning, that things not expressed be comprehended under those that are here expressed. We most humbly supplicate all Kings, Princes, Soveraign Lords, States and Nations, and generally all Persons of what Condition soever to be graciously pleased, that these our lawful and indispensable *Protestations*, which in the simplicity and sincerity of our Hearts we are obliged to make, and do make accordingly, may serve before God, and before them, as a standing Testimony for us and our Posterity, for the Preservation of our Rights, and for the Discharge of our Consciences.

FINIS.

www.ingramcontent.com/pod-product-compliance
Lightning Source LLC
Chambersburg PA
CBHW030119030726
47498CB00007B/2461